Bankruptcy in United States History

Bankruptcy in United States History

BY

CHARLES WARREN

BeardBooks

Washington, DC

THE JULIUS ROSENTHAL FOUNDATION
FOR GENERAL LAW

JULIUS ROSENTHAL, an eminent and beloved member of the Chicago Bar, was born in Germany on September 17, 1828. He pursued his studies at the Universities of Heidelberg and Freiburg, came to Chicago in July, 1854, and was admitted to the bar in 1860. He was especially prominent as a practitioner in the law of wills and in probate and real estate law. As librarian of the Chicago Law Institute from 1867 to 1877 and again from 1888 to 1903, and its president from 1878 to 1880, he was chiefly responsible for its development. He was a member of the first Board of State Law Examiners of Illinois, and its secretary (1897–1899). He died May 14, 1905.

Julius Rosenthal was a lawyer of great learning and rare scholarly attainments. He labored long and earnestly to establish the best standards of legal scholarship. His interest in the welfare of the Law School of Northwestern University was constantly manifested, and of this his numerous gifts of books were tokens.

To honor his memory the University in 1919 established The Julius Rosenthal Foundation for General Law. The income derived from the Foundation is, among other uses, applicable to the cultivation of legal literature, and particularly to the publication of meritorious essays, monographs, and books of a scientific or practical nature concerning the law; to the aid or encouragement of research in the field of legal literature and the preparation for publication of the results of such research; and to the delivery and publication of lectures on subjects concerning the law.

FOREWORD

THIS book is an amplification of the lectures delivered by me at the Law School of Northwestern University, in November, 1934, on the Julius Rosenthal Foundation.

History and law have too long been regarded as distinct subjects, to be treated separately in watertight compartments. In spite of the prominent part which the relations of debtor and creditor have played in our State Legislatures and in Congress throughout our National life, it is a singular fact that each of the great works on American history by McMaster, by Channing, and by Rhodes contains (so far as its index shows) only one cursory reference to bankruptcy; and similarly in the textbooks on the law of that subject, there is little mention of any history connected with bankruptcy legislation. This book is an attempt to place the subject in its proper historical setting.

From the beginning of our National Government, every financial crisis and period of depression has been attended by the passage of stay-laws by State Legislatures, and by pressure on Congress for bankruptcy legislation. From 1793 to 1800, from 1814 to 1827, from 1835 to 1842, from 1860 to 1878, from 1881 to 1898, and during recent years, vigorous debates on bankruptcy have stirred the various Congresses and in them the economic conditions of the times have been vividly depicted. One of the striking features of the history of such economic depressions has been the increase in the scope of the demands for relief through the exercise by Congress of its power under the Bankruptcy Clause of the Constitution. The expansive possibility of this Clause has been one of the most interesting features in the application of our Federal Constitution. At first, relief was demanded only in the interest of the creditor; later, in the interest only of the debtor; but the more recent bankruptcy laws have been regarded as demanded for the National interest in general.

The sketch of the great depressions of the past, and the description of the attempts at legislative adjustment of the relations of debtor and creditor, given in this book, have a bearing upon present conditions and upon future developments of a National economic life. Hence, this book may be of interest to the general reader of history, as well as to the student of economics and to the lawyer, for it presents striking illustrations of the fact that history has often repeated itself in this country. He who is inclined to despond may be encouraged to believe in the adequacy of his own generation and of the Federal Constitution to meet the conditions of the day.

CHARLES WARREN

WASHINGTON, D. C.
June, 1935

CONTENTS

I

THE PERIOD OF THE CREDITOR
1789–1827

THE CONSTITUTION AND BANKRUPTCY

STOCK AND LAND SPECULATIONS AND THE ACT OF 1800

THE SUPREME COURT AND STATE INSOLVENCY LAWS

THE DEPRESSION OF 1819–1824

TEN YEARS OF BANKRUPTCY DEBATE IN CONGRESS

I

THE PERIOD OF THE CREDITOR
1789–1827

BANKRUPTCY is a gloomy and depressing subject. The law of bankruptcy is a dry and discouraging topic. But the history of bankruptcy legislation as seen in the Congressional debates is colorful; for not only does it reflect the changes in viewpoints and in economic conditions in our National history, but it also reminds us of how frequently the views and conditions of today are mere repetitions of the past.

The story of bankruptcy in its connection with our National development can be best told by liberal recourse to the words of those who took an active part in Congressional debates on the subject. While it is true that the Supreme Court has held that such debates are not to be considered in construing a statute, such restriction is a legalism, removing the Court from the realm of actualities.[1] The legal historian, on the other hand, will generally find that it is only from such debates and from the arguments both of opponents and of advocates that he can understand a statute as well as the conditions which produced it. Moreover, it is in such debates that the historian is able to trace the growth of public opinion as to the scope of the United States Constitution. Sixty years

3

ago in an insolvency case in the United States Supreme Court, arising out of the great Chicago fire,
Mr. Justice Miller said: "When we consider the rapid
development of corporations as instrumentalities of
the commercial and business world in the last few
years, with the corresponding necessity of adapting
legal principles to the new and varying exigencies of
this business, it is no solid objection to such a principle that it is modern; for the occasion for it could
not sooner have arisen." [2] In no branch of the law is
there greater necessity for "adapting legal principles
to new and varying exigencies" than in Constitutional law; and nowhere has the Federal Constitution
shown its expansive possibilities more frequently and
more forcibly than in that clause which vests in Congress the power to pass "uniform laws on the subject
of bankruptcies." In using that phraseology, the
founders of the Nation could not define or foresee
the limits of its future application, but in all their
work, they clearly understood that "they were not
building a strait-jacket to restrain the growth and
shackle the spirits of their descendants for all time
to come; they were devising a political instrumentality which, while firm, was nevertheless to be
flexible enough to serve the varying social needs of
changing generations."

As is well known, the subject of bankruptcy was
not considered in the Federal Convention of 1787
until a very late date in its proceedings, when, on
August 29, Charles Pinckney of South Carolina
moved to commit the Full Faith and Credit Clause

4

(Article XVI of John Rutledge's report of the Committee of Detail of August 6) with an addition "to establish uniform laws upon the subject of bankruptcies and respecting the damages arising on the protest of foreign bills of exchange." On September 1, Rutledge reported a recommendation that in Article VII relating to the Legislative Department, there be added after the power "to establish an uniform rule of naturalization throughout the United States," a power "to establish uniform laws on the subject of bankruptcies." On September 3, 1787, this clause was adopted with practically no debate, and with the State of Connecticut alone voting nay — Roger Sherman of that State objecting to any grant of power which would make it possible to punish bankruptcies by death, as had been done by some early laws in England. Gouverneur Morris thought it "an extensive and delicate subject," but "he would agree to it because he saw no danger of abuse by the Legislature of the United States." In the Report of the Committee on Style and in the final draft of the Constitution, this power was inserted immediately after the power to regulate commerce, as Clause 4 of Section 8 of Article I.[3]

The only other action taken by the Convention having a possible bearing upon bankruptcy was on September 14, 1787, when a motion by Nathaniel Gorham was refused a seconding, to place upon Congress the same prohibition as to impairing the obligation of contracts as had been laid upon the States. Had this motion been adopted, no bankruptcy law could have discharged prior debts. It may be noted that the Constitution of the Confederate States of March 11, 1861, contained this precise provision as follows: "The Congress shall have power . . . to establish . . . uniform laws on the subject of bankruptcies, throughout the Confederate States; but no law of Congress shall discharge any debt contracted before the passage of the same." [4] As will be seen *infra*, this was the meaning which Democratic statesmen for seventy years tried to have read into the Bankruptcy Clause of the Federal Constitution.

Whether the framers of the Constitution used the word "bankruptcies" as a compulsory form of proceeding confined to traders as in the English bankruptcy legislation existing in 1787, or whether they contemplated that it might apply to all classes of persons and all forms of insolvency as in some of the American States of that day, are matters as to which for eighty years there was much discussion. When the Federal Constitution was framed, Pennsylvania had an "Act for the Regulation of Bankruptcy" enacted September 16, 1785, applying (as in England) only to merchants and traders and discharging them only from debts contracted after the Act; and that State had also had various acts for the relief of all insolvent debtors. [5] It has been said that Rhode Island had a perfect bankruptcy law in 1787; [6] New York had no bankruptcy law applicable to merchants only, but had an insolvency law applicable to any debtor on consent of three-quarters of his creditors, and discharging debts; and some of the other States had provisions for discharging any insolvent from imprisonment only. Nowhere in the States, other than Pennsylvania, however, does there seem to have been the clear line of demarcation which existed in England between a bankruptcy system and an insolvency system, i.e. between discharge of traders from their debts, and discharge of all persons merely from imprisonment for debt — upon surrender of their property to their creditors.

In contemporary debates or writings, there is no evidence as to the meaning and scope of the Bankruptcy Clause in the Constitution, except that in *The Federalist* (No. 42) James Madison said: "The power of establishing uniform laws of bankruptcy is so intimately connected with the regulation of commerce, and will prevent so many frauds where the parties or their property may lie or be removed into different States that the expediency of it seems not likely to be drawn into question." [7] It is highly probable that the attention of the framers was chiefly centred on bankruptcy in its relation to commerce, and that the exercise of the power was conceived as primarily for the benefit of the commercial class of creditors and debtors, as in England. [8] Yet that fears existed lest the Bankruptcy Clause should be held to include cases of insolvency and to apply to others than merchants and traders is shown by the action of the New York Constitutional Convention in 1788, which urged an amendment to the Federal Constitution so as to provide "that the power of Congress to

7

pass uniform laws concerning bankruptcy shall only extend to merchants and other traders; and that the States respectively may pass laws for the relief of other insolvent debtors."

A steadily expansive interpretation, however, has been given to the Bankruptcy Clause during the one hundred and forty-eight years which have ensued.[9] As long ago as 1837 Senator Thomas H. Benton said: "We are to use our granted powers, according to the circumstances of our own country, and according to the genius of our republican institutions, and according to the progress of events and the expansion of light and knowledge among ourselves. . . . It is *bankruptcies* and not *bankruptcy* that is to be the object of those uniform laws." And it is now substantially settled by legislative practice and by judicial decision (though for many years challenged) that a statute may be "on the *subject* of bankruptcy," without being technically a "bankruptcy law" — in other words, that any National law which deals with inability to pay debts and which is uniform throughout the country is a law "on the subject of bankruptcy." Whatever may have been the anticipation of the framers, the fact is that the Bankruptcy Power has developed steadily, from being a regulation of traders for purely commercial purposes, into a National policy of relief, for creditors and debtors of all classes and for the restoration of business life, with debts adjusted or discharged. Moreover, there has been a steady progress of the idea that these statutory methods of relief should be based on the interest of the

8

Nation at large; and as the particular needs and interests of the Nation change in different periods of distress and disaster, so the exercise of the Bankruptcy Power may be expanded to meet these National needs. Four things stand out strikingly, in our history. First, that every bankruptcy law has been the product of some financial crisis or business depression; second, that from the outset the divisions in Congress over such laws have been largely sectional; third, that there has been a persistent and continuous opposition to a compulsory or involuntary bankruptcy law; and fourth, that, until the decision on May 27, 1935, in the Frazier-Lemke Act case, no development under the Bankruptcy Clause of the Constitution has ever failed of support by the Supreme Court. The trail of that Clause is strewn with a host of unsuccessful objections based on constitutional grounds against the enactment of various provisions, all of which are now regarded as perfectly orthodox features of a bankruptcy law. [10] Thus, it was at first contended that, constitutionally, such a law must be confined to the lines of the English statute; next, that it could not discharge prior contracts; next, that a purely voluntary law would be non-uniform and therefore unconstitutional; next, that any voluntary bankruptcy was unconstitutional; next, that there could be no discharge of debts of any class except traders; next, that a bankruptcy law could not apply to corporations; next, that allowance of State exemptions of property would make a bankruptcy law non-uniform; next, that any composition

9

was unconstitutional; next, that there could be no composition without an adjudication in bankruptcy; next, that there could be no sale of mortgaged property free from the mortgage. All these objections, so hotly and frequently asserted from period to period, were overcome either by public opinion or by the Court.

It was eleven years after the organization of the Government before the Bankruptcy Power granted by the Constitution was exercised by Congress; but it is interesting to note that in the very first session of the 1st Congress, during which only the most necessary subjects of legislation were considered, bankruptcy was one of those subjects; and as early as June 1, 1789, a Committee of the House was named to prepare a bankruptcy bill. At the next session (February, 1790), the subject was laid on the table, since William Smith of South Carolina stated that:

> The present situation of the country was such as to render a general law on this subject a more intricate and perplexing business than the gentleman was aware of. He thought it more prudent to defer the business till the public debt should be funded and banks established, without which it was difficult to conceive how arrangements could be made to facilitate the payments of debts or the operation of such a law. He said that the insolvent acts in the several States would answer for the present.

Before the 2nd Congress adjourned, an alarming panic had swept over the country in 1792, as a result of a wild wave of speculation in Government scrip and in the shares of every kind of corporation —

bank, canal, turnpike, manufacturing, coal and land companies which had been recklessly organized everywhere and whose stock found eager subscribers. Letters of Thomas Jefferson at this time vividly depict the prevalent "appetite for gambling," the "rage for getting rich in a day," "the stockjobbing speculations," "the credit and fate of the Nation seeming to hang on the desperate throws and plunges of gambling scoundrels." [11] Just before "the paper bubble burst," he wrote, in March, 1792:

> This nefarious business is becoming more and more the public detestation, and cannot fail, when the knowledge of it shall be sufficiently extended, to "tumble" its authors headlong from their heights. Money is leaving from the remoter parts of the Union and flowing to this place to purchase paper; and here, a paper medium supplying its place, it is shipped off in exchange for luxuries. The value of property is necessarily falling in the places left bare of money. In Virginia, for instance, property has fallen 25 % in the last twelve months.

In April, when the failure of William Duer, the leading speculator of New York, crashed many others down with him, Jefferson wrote that it was computed that the dead loss at New York was about $5,000,000, "which is reckoned the value of all the buildings of that city, so that if the whole town had been burnt to the ground it would have been the measure of the present calamity"; and in Boston and in Philadelphia, the dead loss was about $1,000,000. The result was, he wrote, that all over the country "building and other improvements are suspended, workmen turned adrift, country produce not to be sold at any price." All this has today a very familiar sound, as has Jefferson's philosophical remark that:

No man of reflection who had ever attended to the South Sea Bubble in England, or that of Law in France, and who applied the lessons of the past to the present time, could fail to foresee the issue tho he might not calculate the moment at which it would happen. . . . All that stuff called scrip, of whatever description, was folly or roguery, and under a resemblance to genuine public paper it buoyed itself up to a par with that. It has given a severe lesson; yet such is the public gullibility in the hands of cunning and unprincipled men, that it is doomed by nature to receive these lessons once in an age at least.[11]

Though a bankruptcy bill was reported in this 2nd Congress in the hope of relieving these conditions and of preventing their repetition, no action was taken; and during the next four years similar bills proposed in the 3rd and 4th Congresses also failed of consideration. [12] In 1797, however, there again arose an insistent demand for a bankruptcy law, owing to another financial crash brought about by the wild over-speculation which had been going on in real estate all over the country — William Duer and his Scioto Associates in Ohio; the Miami Purchase in Ohio of John Cleves Symmes, Jonathan Dayton, and Elias Boudinot; the notorious Yazoo Companies which had bought from the State of Georgia 30,000,000 acres covering most of the present States of Alabama and Mississippi; the North American Land Company owning 6,000,000 acres in New York,

Pennsylvania, and the South, in which Robert Morris, James Greenleaf, Justice James Wilson, and Robert G. Harper were interested; and the tremendous holdings of Morris, Greenleaf, and John Nicholson in District of Columbia lots. Almost all of these projects had resulted in ruin and imprisonment for debt. William Duer died in a debtor's prison in New York; Robert Morris, the great financier of the Revolution, was in the Prune Street Jail in Philadelphia for nearly three years, with debts of about $12,000,000; the distinguished James Wilson, a Justice of the United States Supreme Court, just before his death, went to North Carolina to avoid imprisonment for debt in Pennsylvania; and a like fate had overtaken many other rich and prominent traders.[13] Only a few States had insolvent laws which could discharge prisoners for debt. The need of a National bankruptcy statute, therefore, was gravely felt. Accordingly, such a bill (of 59 sections) was introduced in the 5th Congress in 1798 by Robert G. Harper of South Carolina.[14] It was vigorously debated, and even at this early point in our history it is to be noted that the lines of division were largely geographical and sectional — the North against the South, and the commercial cities against the agricultural regions. As the debate took place in or soon after the excited partisan discussion in Congress over the Alien and Sedition Laws, party divisions on the bankruptcy bill were also apparent. Moreover, as the bill followed closely the existing English Bankrupt Act and applied only to traders, it was purely a creditors' measure; though representatives of the debtor class were influential enough to secure an amendment in their favor, through a motion to strike out a clause which provided that there should be no discharge of debts contracted prior to the Act. As William Craik of Maryland said: [15]

> The only reason which he could suppose might be alleged in favor of this clause was, that it might be thought by some that the Legislature had no right to interfere between a creditor and his debtor, in respect to transactions which took place before the passing of this law. But he was satisfied that no system of bankruptcy could be formed without affecting in some degree the contracts in existence at the time.

And James A. Bayard said:

> When this subject was under consideration in the Committee of the Whole, some gentlemen were of opinion that to pass this law, without a provision, would make it partake of the nature of an *ex post facto* law, which is prohibited by the Constitution. He believed, when it was recollected that the Legislature, for want of a bankrupt law, has passed an insolvent law in order to take persons out of confinement, it would be acknowledged that no objection could lie against a bankrupt law, on account of its interfering between the contracts of debtors and creditors, which would not equally lie against an insolvent law, as without such a law, a man would be obliged to lie in prison all his life, if his debts were not paid. It is true, a bankrupt law discharges a man's property as well as his person, from the power of the creditor; but the thing is the same in both cases. He assumed it as a just principle that when a man gives credit to another, he does it not only subject to the existing laws, but to all others which may be passed.

Harper and Charles Pinckney of South Carolina, Harrison Gray Otis and Samuel Sewall of Massachusetts, and James A. Bayard of Delaware, — all Federalists and representatives of the commercial interests — were the leading advocates of the bill. Strong opposition was made by Anti-federalists from the South and from the agricultural class like Albert Gallatin of Pennsylvania, Abraham Baldwin of Georgia, and William Gordon of New Hampshire. If the law only applied to cities, he would vote for it, said Gallatin, but he could not consent to oppress the country traders by such a system. The fact that the States had not generally passed bankruptcy laws showed that they did not want them. Gordon, in opposing the bill, said that it was not required in "the natural operation of commerce," that it was the product of the "spirit of speculation which had raged to a great extent in this country, which had driven the merchant from his country house to speculate in land and produced a sort of mania among the people of the United States. The consequence is that our jails are crowded with persons anxiously solicitous for an act of this kind." He pointed out that the farmers and country traders would suffer by such an act. Farmers and planters do business on credit, make payments when their crops come in, and frequently are late in payment; and thus the country trader with whom they deal may fail to pay the city merchant promptly, and if the latter proceeds in bankruptcy against the country trader he in turn must press his farmer or planter debtor, with some compulsory process. Hence, a bankruptcy law was unsuited to conditions in this country which were so different from those prevailing in England. The Representatives from Virginia were almost unanimously opposed to a National bankruptcy system; for under it all property of a debtor might be reached by a creditor, whereas under Virginia statutes freehold land could not be taken on execution.[16] This objection had been made by Thomas Jefferson as early as 1792, to the bill then introduced.[17] Writing to his son-in-law, he said: "A bankrupt bill is brought in, in such a form as to render almost all the landholders of this State liable to be declared bankrupts. It assumes a right of seizing and selling lands. Hitherto, we had imagined the General Government could not meddle with the title to lands." And in notes which he then prepared, he said:

The lands of the bankrupt are to be taken, sold, and is this not a predominant question between the General and State Legislatures? Is commerce so much the basis of the existence of the United States as to call for a bankrupt law? On the contrary, are we not almost agricultural? Should not all laws be made with a view essentially to the poor husbandman? When laws are wanting for the particular description of other callings, should the husbandman be carefully excused from their operation, and preserved under that of the general system only, which general system is fitted to the condition of the husbandman?

On the other hand, the advocates of the bill, largely from the commercial sections of the country, pointed out the necessity of restoring to active trade-life the

thousands of debtors then in jail or else unable to
resume business by reason of their load of undis-
charged debts; and they further urged the necessity
of preventing such a condition from again arising.
As Otis of Massachusetts said:

Misfortune, enterprise, speculation and a spirit of over-
trading, have involved thousands in ruin. . . . Men fail for
millions and though these great leviathans of speculation,
after sunk in the ocean for a time, may rise again and
revel on the surface, yet the widows and orphans, the fair
merchants, industrious tradesmen, and credulous friends,
who are involved in the same whirlpool, rise no more. To
prevent these mischiefs, we should give to creditors a control over the property of their debtors, so as to stop the
fraudulent in their careers, and we should rescue the honest
and unfortunate insolvent from the oppression of a vindic-
tive creditor.

James A. Bayard of Delaware said that "wherever
there is an extensive commerce, extensive credit must
necessarily be given." A bankrupt law he held was
necessary to protect creditors from dishonest and
fraudulent debtors, as well as to enable creditors to
protect honest debtors whose trade had been sub-
jected to unforeseen accidents who shall surrender
all their property in order to obtain a discharge. He
felt that a bankruptcy system might prevent, in the
future, conditions such as then prevailed: "We have
seen men going on in speculative schemes, by means
of fictitious credit, imposing upon the community and
amassing property by contracting debts to an immense extent without an intention to pay, and ultimately failing, to the ruin of thousands of indi-

17

viduals." One argument made by Bayard was undoubtedly potent in lining up political opposition; for he concluded his speech with these words, of a Federalist character little likely to please the Jeffersonian party.[18]

This law, he trusted, would also have an effect to unite and nationalize the United States and its permanent operation will cement together the different parts of the Union and connect more closely the Nation with the Federal Government. He could not help thinking that this view of the subject furnishes the true ground of Gallatin's opposition. Gentlemen will not say that I mean to make this a political question, for in doing this, he did not know but he might lose more than he should gain; but believing it would have this political effect, he thought proper to suggest the idea. He considered the present bill among the greatest National objects.

The bill, having been lost by a close vote in the 5th Congress, was again reported by Bayard in the House in the next Congress in 1799. The need of such a law had now become urgent; for, on top of the financial ruin caused by the land speculators, had come the commercial losses due to captures of our vessels by the French in what our Supreme Court termed our "limited, imperfect war with France in 1799." Business failures involving large amounts had occurred in New York, Philadelphia, and Baltimore. As Jefferson wrote to Madison: "The whole commercial race are lying on their oars and gathering in their affairs, not knowing what new failure may put their resources to the proof." In the existing stagnation of commerce, he said, loans could not be made

18

or money transferred from one city to another.[19] A motion that the bill should not apply to prior debts was rejected (Bayard and John Marshall voting against it); and the bill was finally passed in the House, February 21, 1800, with the casting vote of the Speaker (Theodore Sedgwick of Massachusetts) by a vote of 49 to 48, representing almost wholly a partisan and geographical division. In the Senate, a motion coming from Southern Senators that "this Act shall not be construed to extend to farmers, graziers, drivers, tavern-keepers or manufacturers" was lost by a party vote of 12 to 14, and the bill was passed by a vote of 16 to 12.[20]

This first Bankrupt Act of 1800 was by its terms limited to a five years' operation, but it only lasted three years. As early as January, 1803, a move was made in the House for its repeal [21]; and in November, 1803, a repeal Act was passed by the heavy majorities of 99 to 13 in the House and 17 to 12 in the Senate, though only after a very vigorous fight by the advocates of the law, principally by James A. Bayard. While in later years it was stated on many occasions in Congress that the repeal was a Jeffersonian party measure, there is little basis for the charge.[22] The dissatisfaction with the law had been very general — based on several grounds. First there was the difficulty of travel to the distant and unpopular Federal Courts.[23] Second, very small dividends had been paid to creditors, as most of the debtors petitioned into bankruptcy were already in jail. Third, the Act had been largely used by rich debtors and speculators, and in some cases by fraudulent debtors, to obtain discharge from their debts and start their operations afresh. As was said a few years later: "We saw men rich today, bankrupt tomorrow, and next day in full business and great style, while the poor farmer or manufacturer who had been ruined by their extravagance must suffer the penalties of the law in a jail." Incidentally, among the prominent debtors released was Robert Morris after nearly three years in jail.

Though, technically, a bankruptcy proceeding could only be initiated by creditors and was a compulsory process, actually it was utilized by debtors themselves through some friendly creditor.[24] As was said in the debate:

There was no weight in the remark that the commission was taken out at the instance of the creditor, as that was merely a nominal act, the creditor usually being made use of who was the friend of the bankrupt. That it operated to the benefit of the debtor was clear from its liberating all his future acquisitions. . . . That hence sprang up a tenfold temptation to fraud over that which existed under the common insolvent laws. . . . Fraud once successfully perpetrated and concealed, every restraint is removed. . . . Evils infinitely greater have been inflicted in inconsiderate and fraudulent debtors taking refuge in the provisions of the bankruptcy law than from all the inhumanity exercised by merciless creditors over unfortunate debtors.

The number of cases begun under the law was in fact extremely small — not over 500 in Pennsylvania, New York, Maryland, and the District of Columbia, the four places where most advantage was taken of the law — but the sentiment aroused against the Act was quite disproportionate to its actual effects.[25]

The sense of injury of the agricultural class was undoubtedly one of the chief causes of opposition, particularly in the South. John Randolph of Virginia said that he "knew by experience that many planters had been choused out of their property by the operations of this ruinous law." It is "a partial, immoral, and impolitic law, anti-Republican and opposed to the principles of our Government," said Thomas Newton, Jr., of Virginia. John Bacon of Massachusetts said that Bayard, the leading advocate of the Act, was "better acquainted with the interest of merchants than of the cultivators of the soil." Others urged that it was unjust as favoring one class of citizens, the traders, at the expense of all other classes. They cited the common case of a merchant availing himself of the benefits of bankruptcy and thereby cancelling the demands of the mechanic or the farmer who might be his creditors, and of the same individual mechanic or farmer remaining debtors of another merchant with their property subject to his seizure at any period of their life. They preferred the State insolvent systems which extended relief to all classes of insolvent debtors. Opponents of repeal admitted that the Act was an experiment and imperfect in many respects, and needed amendments; but their pleas that it might be given a further chance to operate were overruled.[26]

As an illustration of the fact that desire for bankruptcy legislation and depression have always been coupled in our history, it may be noted that repeal of the law caused less practical hardship at the time than had been expected, by reason of the fact of the revival of commercial prosperity for a few years after 1800. The French depredations had temporarily ceased and neutral traders were enriched, as the United States became the carriers and suppliers of Europe. Exports had increased from $19,000,000 in 1791 to $94,000,000 in 1801 (and to $61,000,000 in 1811).[27] But after 1806, a great change was produced by the French Decrees and English Orders in Council, under which our ships suffered severe losses and confiscations; in addition, the Embargo and Non-intercourse Acts under Presidents Jefferson and Madison were the cause of widespread ruin to the traders of New England and New York. Debts piled up; the jails were filled to overflowing with imprisoned debtors; and in consequence renewed demands were made upon Congress in 1809, and again in 1812, for another bankruptcy law; but action on the petition was refused, for again the South and the farmers were opposed. John Smilie of Pennsylvania said that "every honest man abhorred the bankruptcy system"; Thomas Newton, Jr., of Virginia, said that we had already had "unequivocal experience of its bad effects."[28]

Further violent commercial disturbances, however, were now being caused by the War of 1812; and in the midst of these conditions, the commercial public (in April, 1814) were seriously alarmed by a decision rendered by Justice Bushrod Washington in the

United States Circuit Court; for he held a State insolvent law of Pennsylvania unconstitutional, not only because it discharged prior contracts but also on the ground that Congress had sole and exclusive power to pass any law discharging debtors.[29] If this decision should be affirmed by the Supreme Court, all State insolvent laws would fall to the ground; and unless Congress should act, there would be no way in which any debtor anywhere could get relief from imprisonment or a discharge from his debts. Creditors and debtors alike, in New York, Philadelphia, Boston, and Baltimore, urgently petitioned Congress to remedy such a situation. "They look to Congress alone for relief from the difficulties into which they have been plunged and by whom alone they can be relieved if the recent decision of the Circuit Court be confirmed," said John W. Taylor of New York.[30] Congress, however, refused to take any action either in 1815 or in 1816, although in the latter year Rufus King of New York referred to the seriousness of the Pennsylvania decision, and spoke again of the embargo, which had been "of so little importance against an enemy and so cruel an operation to the suffering merchants and tradesmen." [31] In April, 1817, a decision by Justice Brockholst Livingston in the United States Circuit Court in New York, upholding the New York insolvent law of 1811 and differing from Justice Washington's decision, gave the merchants some hope; and in 1818, an elaborate bill of 54 pages reported by Joseph Hopkinson of Philadelphia in the House, was exhaustively debated in the 15th Congress, but was again defeated by a vote of 82 to 70.[32] Once more the South and the country Democrats, and for the first time Western representatives, rose in opposition.

A year after this defeat, came the decision by the Supreme Court of the noted case of *Sturges* v. *Crown-inshield*, in which, in 1819, Chief Justice Marshall held the New York State insolvent law of 1811 unconstitutional as applied to prior contracts. This decision, followed on the same day by a decision holding a Louisiana insolvent law of 1808 invalid,[33] produced consternation throughout the mercantile community; for owing to a misunderstanding of the Chief Justice's language, and to a misstatement by the Reporter of the *per curiam* decision in the Louisiana case, it was thought, both by lawyers and laymen and by various State Courts, that the Supreme Court had decided that under the Constitution no State had power to pass any insolvent law, either as to prior or as to future contracts.[34] The decision appeared the more serious by reason of the fact that, at that time, it was believed by most statesmen that Congress had no power to pass a bankrupt law except for traders. Hence, if neither the States nor Congress could give a remedy for other classes of insolvent debtors, the outlook was black indeed. "The decision has excited extensive alarm in this community," said the *New York Evening Post*. "No decision has ever been made," said another New York paper, "which came more immediately home to the business and feelings of the community than such a one as

this is supposed to be." A Georgia paper said: "What
are wretched debtors to do? The States can exempt
nothing but their bodies from the harassing pursuit
of the law; the Congress in making a bankrupt law
will include only the trading class. There must,
nevertheless, be power somewhere to free debtors
from the load of obligations under which they must
labor." And a Baltimore paper said: "The decision
renders the passage of a National law imperious.
The apathy that prevails in Congress on the subject
is really surprising. How long will they shut their
ears against the cries of distress? How long will they
neglect supplications of thousands?" [35]

Moreover, this decision, destroying at once all hope
of relief by State laws to those who were then in debt,
came at a particularly distressing time; for the country was suffering from the severest depression it had
ever undergone, resulting from an accumulation of
causes — the confiscation of American vessels during
our neutrality; the War of 1812; the flood of imported
goods after the war, demoralizing our markets; the
fall in price of our own produce in Europe in 1818 and
1819; the State bank failures; and the reckless conduct and extravagant expansion of loans by the Bank
of the United States, followed by its contraction of
credits; the fifty per cent diminution in our circulation of currency from 1815 to 1819 — all, as one
Congressman termed them, "so many stages on the
road to ruin." [36] As Senator Benton wrote later: [37]

The years 1817 and 1820 were a period of gloom and
agony, no money, either gold or silver; no paper converti-

ble into specie; no measure or standard of value left remaining. . . . No price for property or produce. No sales but those of the sheriff or marshal. No purchasers at the execution sales but the creditor or some hoarder of money. No employment for industry — no demand for labor . . . no medium of exchange but depreciated paper. . . . Distress, the universal cry of the people. Relief, the universal demand, thundered at the doors of all Legislatures, State or Federal.

"The years 1819, 1820 and 1821," said James Buchanan in the Senate, "were the most disastrous which the country had ever experienced since the adoption of the Federal Constitution. Not only merchants and speculators were then involved, but the rage for speculation had extended to the farmers and mechanics throughout the country and had rendered vast numbers of them insolvent." [38] In August, 1819, *Niles Register* said: "There are 20,000 persons daily seeking work in Philadelphia . . . in New York, 10,000 able-bodied men are said to be wandering the streets daily looking for work. . . . In Baltimore, there may be about 10,000 persons in unsteady employment or actually suffering because they cannot get into business." During the winter of 1819–1820, soup kitchens were established in several of the larger cities. In the country, the wheat crops of several years had been essentially injured and in some instances almost destroyed. Prices were in a complete state of collapse. Cotton fell fifty per cent between January and June, 1819. To prevent sacrifice of debtors' property, stay-laws and appraisal-laws were enacted in Tennessee, Kentucky, Missouri, and

Ohio; and many other States established a loan office for relief of debtors.

Under these circumstances, it was natural that strong pressure for some form of relief should be again brought upon Congress. In 1820–1821, a bankruptcy bill of 64 sections (53 pages) was introduced in the Senate of the 16th Congress; and there then arose a contest which lasted for twenty years. Heretofore, the only bankruptcy system known in England or in this country was one applicable to traders alone, and one in which action must originate with the creditor. Now, for the first time in the history of the world, legislation was proposed to benefit debtors at large, instead of merely to enable creditors to reach the property of merchants and traders. The contest was initiated by Nicholas Van Dyke of Delaware, through a motion to amend the original bill by providing that any person imprisoned for debt might voluntarily file a petition to be adjudged a bankrupt. This was an entirely unheard of and novel proposal; but, largely as a result of a strong speech in its favor by Henry Clay of Kentucky, the amendment was finally adopted by the Senate by a vote of 25 to 16.[39] This action, however, caused the rejection of the whole bill by a vote of 15 to 23, through a combination of Northern Senators (who believed that a bankruptcy law was unconstitutional unless confined to merchants and traders) with Southerners (who were opposed to any bankruptcy law at all). In the second session of this 16th Congress, the Senate passed a bill by a vote of 19 to 18, after an attempt to insert a voluntary bankruptcy provision had failed; but the House did not act. And there were many men who agreed with John Quincy Adams, who wrote in his Diary that, to relieve the universal distress, "Government can do nothing, at least nothing by any measure yet proposed, but transfer discontents and propitiate one class . . . by disgusting another. . . . As it is, the arbiters of weal and woe, the healers and destroyers, Time and Chance, must bring the catastrophe or the cure." [40]

In the next (17th) Congress, in 1822, a tremendous struggle took place in the House to pass a bankruptcy law confined to traders (to be in force for only three years). "There are more insolvent debtors than ever before," said John Sergeant of Pennsylvania, who had drafted the bill. Again an amendment was proposed and adopted to allow voluntary bankruptcy by all debtors (this time, however, with the limitation that the assent of a majority of creditors must be obtained), but its adoption cost the bill its life; for a combination of Senators who opposed all bankruptcy bills with those Senators who believed that such a bill must be confined to merchants and traders, and with those Senators who objected to any restriction on a debtor's right voluntarily to become bankrupt, again defeated the bill.[41] The Southern and Western states voted almost solidly against the measure. "Thus perish the hopes of thousands of honest, industrious, enterprising, and virtuous citizens who have borne for years the deprivations and hardships of severe adversity," said a New York paper.[42] A contemporary writer was of the opinion that, being a Northern measure, part of the hostility to it was due to the fact that it was debated during the period when so great heat had been engendered by the contests over "that ill-starred, useless source of irritation," — the admission of Missouri to the Union.[43] The same writer also said:

> I am persuaded that it is, and must continue to be, impracticable to carry a bankrupt bill which is confined to the trading classes. On that rock, the bill was wrecked at a time when public expectation was at the highest pitch of anxiety and when the very hall of legislation was inundated with memorials and petitions for a bankrupt law. It appears to me, therefore, that the question, practically, is merely this — whether it is better to have no bankrupt law at all, or to have one of which, in some shape or other, all classes of the community may alike have the benefit and protection. The bankrupt bills heretofore introduced have been uniformly modelled on the English bankrupt system. That spell of reverence which benumbs the senses and blunts the acuteness of almost all professional men in regard to the faults and absurdities of the English common law seems to have operated, in some degree, on the minds of those distinguished lawyers who have successively attempted to introduce the English bankrupt law into our own country.

And this writer continued: "There exists, in Congress, it is well known, a most violent prejudice against a bankrupt law in any shape whatever; and an opposition of discordant reasons but united purpose has always been arrayed against any exercise of the power by Congress to pass a bankrupt law."

It is interesting to note some of these greatly divergent arguments in opposition to the various bills from
1818 to 1822. Primarily, the Senators and Congressmen from Virginia and South Carolina urged with
vehemence the unconstitutionality of the bills, on the
grounds, first, that Congress could not, and should
not, pass a retrospective bill affecting prior contracts;
and second, that Congress could not pass an insolvency law, i.e. a law applying to the debts of other
than traders. Their arguments in favor of inviolabil-
ity of contracts were strong on the moral but weak
on the legal side; [44] for all English bankruptcy laws,
at the time of the Constitution and since, had applied
to existing contracts. As Cadwallader Colden of
New York said: [45]

It is a very unexpected ground to tell the people that
the Constitution which they have given us is not to be
considered as the supreme law of the land because its
precepts are, in our opinion, a violation of the laws of God.
I think our constituents will be very likely to inquire
whether we are so superior to those who framed the Constitution as to be better judges than they were of the obligations of morality.

And Joshua Cushman of Maine said that many who
conceded the Constitutional right still contended
that [46]

the superior obligations of morality and religion be placed
as insuperable barriers. On this head, I have to remark,
what all history evinces, that when those who should be
statesmen leave their proper functions and turn philosophers and mere religionists, there is reason to tremble for

the safety of the Government and the liberties of the people. Who, more than the philosophers of France, furnished the materials for the bloody tragedy? . . . And who but the godly party in England . . . put down one branch of the Legislature, beheaded the Supreme Executive, and established a military despotism?

James Buchanan of Pennsylvania was especially concerned as to the moral aspect of permitting any class other than merchants to be discharged from their debts; and, especially, said he:

Leave the agricultural interest pure and uncorrupted, and they will forever form the basis on which the Constitution and liberties of your country may safely repose. Do not, I beseech you, teach them to think lightly of the solemn obligation of contracts. No Government on earth, however corrupt, has ever enacted a bankrupt law for farmers. It would be a perfect monster in this country, where our institutions depend altogether upon the virtue of the people. . . . Such a provision would spread a moral taint through society which would corrupt it to its very core. Legislative experiments should be tried with extreme caution. An act may expire in three years by its own limitation — yet its pernicious influence may last for ages. If, by expunging a law from your statute books, you could efface its effects from the human mind or withdraw its influence from the human character, then indeed experiments in politics would be as harmless as those in philosophy. This, however, is not the case.

Advocates of the bill replied to the constitutional arguments on their merits; but they also alleged that the Constitution was being put forward too frequently as an obstacle to progress. Ralph I. Lockwood of New York wrote, about this time, in a work

31

on the bankruptcy law, that he regretted "that that sacred instrument should be so often and so lightly perverted, for the purpose of creating difficulties and opposition when all other resources of argument have failed. It seems, of late, as if nothing in that instrument could stand the test of modern ingenuity. It is a nose of wax in the hands of some gentlemen who can always make it into just what fashion it pleases them." [47] To comments of this kind, Andrew Stevenson of Virginia replied that he was "one of the few who believed that constitutionality and expediency did not mean the same thing" and that the Constitution should be expounded "with a jealous eye to the rights and objects it was intended to secure and not as policy or power might direct"; [48] but, he said, "I am well aware, from what I have seen and heard, that discussions upon Constitutional law and the powers of the General Government are not very graciously received in this House, and especially by those gentlemen who would be glad to see the powers of the Federal Government enlarged."

The violent opposition by John Randolph and most of the Virginia representatives was largely due to the fact that a National bankruptcy law would enable creditors to reach all real estate of their debtor, whereas under the Virginia State law real estate in fee could not be taken by a creditor on execution.[49] "The secret of Virginia opposition is, they are not willing to subject their land to be sold for payment of just debts," said Samuel Smith of Maryland.[50] Randolph's objection to this bill, said John

McPherson Berrien of Georgia, is that "it will apply the axe to the root of the freehold system of Virginia." And Joseph Hopkinson of Pennsylvania said in reply to Henry St. George Tucker of Virginia: "If there be any privileged order of citizens among us, it is these same landholders of Virginia who alone can vote in their State." To this charge of self-interested motives on the part of Virginians, William S. Archer retorted that such a motive was not confined to that State: "Whether bank bills or tariff bills or bankrupt bills, the demand has but one source, the influence of some private interest or distress. Public good is an inactive, lethargic principle whose still, small voice is never heard in clamor." [51]

In addition to Virginia and South Carolina, opposition came from other Southern States, based on their rigid views as to any extension of the power and jurisdiction of the Federal Government and its courts. Moreover, the agricultural class in the South and North were very generally antagonistic, believing that any bankruptcy law was unsuited to the United States, since it was not a commercial country; [52] and the representatives of this class contended that such a law was intended for the benefit of and discriminated in favor of merchants, granted exclusive rights to them, and created a "privileged order." To this last extravagant argument, the upholders of the bill replied that "a privileged order composed of bankrupts is laughable," and that if there was any such order, it was the "Order of Misery." [53]

One reason why the bill was regarded as discriminatory does not appear on the face of it, and is rarely referred to in the old law books — viz., that while a bankruptcy law on the lines of the English statutes or on those of the American Act of 1800 ostensibly provided only for involuntary bankruptcy initiated against a debtor by his creditors, in actual operation such a law permitted what was tantamount to voluntary bankruptcy through the initiation of proceedings by a friendly creditor at the request of his debtor — and so a practical privilege of concealed voluntary bankruptcy was reserved to merchants and traders only, under all bills drafted on the English model. No wonder that there soon arose in this country pressure from all debtor classes for a bill providing for actual, open, voluntary bankruptcy! But while attacking any bankruptcy law based on the English system and confined to traders, they argued equally strongly that no bankruptcy law should ever be extended compulsorily to farmers, planters, and mechanics. They also pointed out, as a specific instance of injury caused by the English type of law, the fact that country traders indebted to city merchants could be discharged of their debts in bankruptcy, but that farmers and planters owing the country trader had to pay their debts in full.

In reply to arguments as to discrimination in favor of the commercial class, advocates of the bill said, but with no success in carrying conviction to the opponents, that any bill which benefited the commercial class equally benefited agriculture, but they

agreed that it would be "utterly impolitic and unjust" to extend the bill specifically to farmers. Thus,
Ezekiel Whitman of Massachusetts said: [54]

These privileges, if conferred, would injure no other
class. . . . On the contrary, in my opinion, the conferring
these privileges will ultimately tend much more to the
benefit of the public than of the merchant. It is the agri-
culturist that will finally reap the benefit of the measure. I
agree that the agricultural interest in this country is paramount to all others; and above all ought to be cherished.
It is from the agriculturists that we derive the articles of
primary importance and necessity. This class of men com-
poses at least 9/10 of the population, and the most worthy
population of our country. Their interest is, therefore, in
whatever we do to be first consulted. But, sir, it may be
laid down as a fixed principle, of which there can be no
doubt, that whatever encourages commerce is beneficial to
agriculture. They go hand in hand. . . . If the merchant is
unsuccessful, the farmer can have no ready market for this
surplus product. . . . Hence it becomes our duty to do
everything in our power for the encouragement and protection of the merchant, with a single eye to the prosperity
of the agriculture of our country.

And Joseph Hemphill of Pennsylvania said that the
bill was no injury to farmers: [55]

The landed was the leading interest in this country; and
any measure that would be injurious to that, cannot, in the
end, be beneficial to the nation. It stood, however, in no
danger from legislation in Congress; it was too powerfully
represented; the owners of the soil will always hold the
reins of Government in their own hands; but are not they,
interested in commerce? The merchants are their carriers
and give value to their products. The country was greatly

indebted to commerce for its rapid advancement and prosperity. . . . Is it not politic in the farmers to foster, by every reasonable encouragement, so useful a class of citizens? . . .

Opponents of the bill also claimed that it was not desirable that any bankruptcy law should be uniform throughout the country; and, said James Pindall of Virginia, "this passion for uniformity over the Continent, from Maine to the Mexican Gulf, which is coming so much in vogue, may be pregnant with untried evils. . . . State Legislatures are more intimately acquainted with the will and wants of their constituents." [56]

On the other hand, the bill's advocates pointed out the diversity and complications of the State laws as to attachments and other liens on land properly subject to judgment, and the diversity of the State laws also as to preferences, stay and replevin laws, imprisonment, debt discharge in insolvency, etc., whereby no creditor, whether a merchant or a planter or a farmer, could be sure of non-discriminatory treatment outside of his own State.[57]

One particular argument addressed to Kentucky debtors and creditors was strongly appealing. In that State, laws requiring creditors to accept State bank paper or lands at an appraised value were in force in the State Courts, but under the Federal Process Acts were not in force in the Federal Courts. Hence outside creditors, especially the obnoxious Bank of the United States, were enabled to collect their judgments in gold, silver, and land, while local creditors could not. This was an injustice to Kentucky creditors and debtors alike which a National bankruptcy law could obviate.

An interesting and rather unique argument for extension of the bill to others than traders was made in 1821 by Senator Harrison Gray Otis of Massachusetts, urging that something must be done for the debtor class, by giving them a limited provision for voluntary bankruptcy; otherwise, said he: [58]

What may be expected when their numbers shall be increased and they seriously commence a system of measures for obtaining that relief by their active efforts, which is denied to their supplications? What could be more appalling and inauspicious to men of property, and to Government itself, than to see organized self-created corporations of debtors embodied in all the great commercial towns and formed into one vast combination, to influence elections! What state of things more dangerous than an universal alliance among all classes of debtors, public and private, to effectuate their own freedom through the instrumentality of persons chosen into Congress with no other recommendation? How should you be pleased, sir, to see the great commercial States represented in the Senate by delegates from an established order of insolvent debtors?

This suggestion, over one hundred years ago, of the possibility of a union among debtors to secure representation in Congress is a striking prophecy.

Three years elapsed after 1822 before any further effort was made for bankruptcy legislation; but the depression which started in 1819 still continued to such an extent that in 1824 the Speaker of the House,

Henry Clay, described the situation in terms which sound extremely familiar today:[59]

> In casting our eyes around us, the most prominent circumstance which fixes our attention and challenges our deepest regret is the general distress which pervades the whole country. It is forced upon us by numerous facts of the most incontestable character. It is indicated by the diminished exports of native produce, by the repressed and reduced state of our foreign navigation, by our diminished commerce, by successive unthreshed crops of grain perishing in our barns and barnyards for the want of a market; by the alarming diminution of the circulation medium; by the numerous bankruptcies . . . by an universal complaint of the want of employment and by a consequent reduction of the wages of labor . . . by the reluctant resort to the perilous use of paper money; by the intervention of legislation in the delicate relations of debtor and creditor; and above all, by the low and depressed state of the value of almost every description of the whole mass of the property of the nation, which has, on the average, sunk not less than fifty per cent within a few years. This distress pervades every part of the Union, every class of society, all feel it. It is like the atmosphere which surrounds us — all must inhale it and none can escape it. . . . I have exaggerated nothing. Perfect fidelity to the original would have authorised me to have thrown a deeper and darker hue.

There were men in those days, as today, who doubted whether the country could pull out from these conditions. Others believed that relief must come from Congress, and to mitigate the situation Daniel Webster offered, in the House, a resolution for a National bankruptcy law; but again Congress failed to act.

In the next year (1825), a great debate on the bill for abolition of imprisonment for debt, pressed by Senator Richard M. Johnson of Kentucky, furnished another opportunity for bringing up the subject of bankruptcy; and Senator Robert Y. Hayne of South Carolina reported a very long bill of 94 Sections (78 pages) based on the Senate bill of 1821 and on the new British Revised Bankruptcy Law of 1825. It contained a modified semi-voluntary bankruptcy provision under which any person might be petitioned into bankruptcy on application of his creditors, *but only with the consent of the debtor*; for, said Hayne, "the Committee was aware that the fate of this, as of past bills, may depend on the question whether they shall be extended to persons other than traders." Involuntary bankruptcy, however, even under this bill, was still technically confined to merchants and traders. The pressing necessity for the bill's passage was urged by Hayne, for, he said, the last two years had been "fruitful of the most calamitous events in the commercial world." John McPherson Berrien of Georgia, in support of the bill, said that in the past twenty years the merchants "have passed through a period of commercial calamity to which neither here nor in Europe has there been found a parallel in history." Nevertheless, there were violent objections made to the bill by John Randolph of Virginia and many others, especially as to the constitutionality of voluntary bankruptcy. As to this, Hayne made the interesting reply, that he had no doubt that the Supreme Court would sustain it; and he added that

39

after preparing this bill, it was submitted to one of the ablest Judges of that Bench, who, after a careful examination, suggested several amendments but made no objection to this (voluntary) clause. I hold in my hand a printed sketch of a bankrupt bill, prepared a year since by another able member of that Bench, in which he himself proposes a system of voluntary bankruptcy similar to this.[60] [The Judge referred to was Joseph Story.]

In spite of Hayne's able arguments, the bill was laid on the table, owing to the lateness of the session.[61]

At the next session of the Senate, in 1826–1827, Hayne again introduced his bill (with a five-year limit). He stated that "unfavorable opinions in other parts of the Union were wearing away," and that the bill now excited "deep and grave interest in the public mind." Senator William Henry Harrison of Indiana said the farmers of Ohio and of the West were coming to favor a bill as in their interest, if voluntary. Again a very limited form of voluntary bankruptcy was proposed (Section 93), under which a creditor might petition into bankruptcy persons other than traders, with the assent of the debtor. This provision was intended to remove the charge that the legislation discriminated in favor of the mercantile and against the agricultural class. Moreover, as John Holmes of Maine pointed out, "we have now a large community of manufacturers who are not exactly merchants and who were entitled to bankruptcy relief."

Violent attacks were made by Martin Van Buren of New York and many others on the inclusion of the provision, on the ground that it constituted an insolvency and not a bankruptcy law; that only the States had power to pass insolvent laws; and that exercise of the power by Congress was an unwarrantable Federal aggrandizement — "a new experiment upon the history of all past legislation, immolating the rights of the States." Senator Philip Reed of Maryland indulged in the following language, familiar to our ears today:

Are the States really, as was predicted, to become humble corporations? . . . Already the eyes of the People from the Mississippi to the Bay of Fundy are turned to this magnificent central Government. They see palaces and splendid domes consecrated to the uses of the Legislative and Executive functionaries, and those things cannot be "without their special wonder." It strikes them as the work of magic — many of us being insensible of the means by which these wonderful works of art are erected. Many of us little dream, remote from the scene of political operations, that the money for all this is drawn from the pockets of the people. . . . The innate tendency of this Government is to accumulate political power in the focus of affairs. Such has been the tendency of every Government.

And William Smith of South Carolina stated that "nothing but a fragment of that sacred instrument, the Constitution, now remained; but he hoped the time had not yet arrived when the caprice of public assemblies and the interest of private funds were to establish the rules for construing it." Senator Littleton Waller Tazewell of Virginia and Senator Levi Woodbury of New Hampshire saw in the bill "a dangerous experiment — a vortex of disaster and diffi-

41

culty to State rights and State independence." And Woodbury asked: "What farmer in the Federal Convention of 1787 ever dreamed that he was conferring such a power on Congress over anybody but merchants?" John Branch of North Carolina, who was opposed to any bankruptcy bill, said that he "represented a plain sort of people, was one of them, and a friend of the agricultural portion of the community — those who had been borne down by misfortunes and still more by the merchants and bankers for whom the bill was to be passed." He said that the voluntary section was only "the sugar to disguise the bitterness of the pill to be prescribed to the community."

In support of the bill, it was argued that the State insolvent laws were inadequate, full of injustices, allowing preferences which were invariably made by the insolvent merchant in favor of his bank or commercial creditor, and allowing in New England local creditors to obtain unfair advantages by its system of mesne attachment, so that, as Hayne said, "a distant farmer or planter stands no chance." It was urged that the voluntary section of the bill would benefit the farmer debtor, while the involuntary section would help the farmer creditor; and as to this latter section, Hayne said:

It is said that a commercial bankrupt law will be a fraud upon farmers and planters. . . . I consider agriculture as the first interest in this country — first in magnitude, first in importance — true interests of agriculture cannot be opposed to those of commerce . . . these two great interests mutually support each other. Show me a regulation by

which commerce is to be advanced (I speak not of boun-
ties) and you show me that by which agriculture is to be
promoted. Embarrass your shipping interest and the farmer
feels the increased freight in the diminution of his produce.
Impose heavy duties upon imports and he pays an addi-
tional price for his supplies, . . . and the planter finds his
produce left upon his hands. The stoppage of a bank, the
failure of an extensive mercantile house, the bursting of
any commercial bubble in one of our cities, is felt, though
it may never be heard of, at the very foot of the mountains.
Improving therefore the condition of the merchant, we
essentially improve the condition of the farmer.

An attempt was made to make the bill more palat-
able to the agricultural community and to allay the
strong prejudice against banks, by Branch of North
Carolina, who moved to extend the bill to all banking
establishments, whether incorporated or not. "Let
us coerce," he said, "these associations, which wield
the moneyed destinies of the country, into the practice of justice and fairness . . . by making the bill
instrumental in restraining those arbitrary, and, I
might say, aristocratical moneyed institutions now,
in one sense, privileged beyond the pale of the law."
Barton of Missouri and Smith of South Carolina
agreed that the "abuses of the moneyed institutions
must in some manner be checked." Other strong
Democrats like Hayne, Holmes of Maine, Rowan of
Kentucky, and Van Buren of New York were opposed to any such infringement of State Rights. Van
Buren (who only ten years later was destined to reverse his view entirely) said that to strip a State of
the power of regulating its own chartered banks, and

thus to direct it as to the manner in which it should exercise its sovereignty, was "an odious exercise of power not granted by the Constitution." The amendment was rejected by a vote of 12 to 35.

It is of singular interest to note that Hayne in his bill anticipated by forty-eight years the inclusion of a composition provision in a bankruptcy bill. This section which was introduced as an amendment and accepted by the Senate, he described as follows: [62]

The last amendment offered was a new section, a clause entirely new to this country. Its object was to institute a composition between the bankrupt and the creditors . . . that no such agreement should be consummated without 2/3 of the creditors in value and number agree to accept it. This provision was said to have been found highly advantageous in England, and he looked upon it as promising great benefits. Where the creditors were satisfied that a bankrupt had acted honorably, had not endeavored to retain from them their just debts, and convinced that he had placed within their power all the property of which he was possessed, there certainly seemed no objection to a settlement, by which the debtor, *without the intervention of the law*, could be divested of his property and receive a release from his creditors. There could be no possible objection, supposing all the creditors to join in the composition; the only question was, whether the act of a part of those holding demands could be considered binding upon all. To make the composition dependent upon all the creditors, would be to render it almost entirely abortive; as it was next to impossible that, whatever preliminary steps were taken, the whole number could be assembled together; some would be prevented by absence, others by indisposition, and a variety of causes would operate to prevent the composition, and even when assembled, the

44

consent of the whole would be doubtful. In every country where to compound required the presence of all the creditors, it was attended with great difficulty, almost equal to the non-existence of the provisions. In France, in particular, it was found to be always impracticable to collect all the creditors together, so much so that the system was entirely inoperative. In this country, it appeared to the Committee that 3/4 of the amount and number . . . would be a sufficient portion of the whole. . . . In England, rather more was required. . . .

All this conflict of views, which has been thus briefly sketched above, resulted in much legislative maneuvering in the Senate for over a month in January and February, 1827. A motion to strike out the much debated voluntary section was defeated, whereupon the bill itself was rejected by a vote of 15 to 25 by a combination of those who wanted only an involuntary bill and of those Democrats who opposed any bankruptcy bill. Then on reconsideration, the voluntary section was eliminated by a vote of 34 to 12, whereupon those who favored this section combined with those who opposed any bill, and again defeated the measure on February 6, 1827, by a vote of 21 to 27. And so, after a ten years' struggle in Congress the debtors lost their fight. And it may fairly be said that the weight of legal opinion at that date was against the constitutionality of voluntary bankruptcy in any National law. It was thirteen years before the contest was resumed, after the Panic of 1837 had crashed over the land.

II

THE PERIOD OF THE DEBTOR
1827–1861

THE SUPREME COURT AGAIN

THE PANIC OF 1837 AND THE BANKS

THE FIGHT FOR VOLUNTARY BANKRUPTCY

WHIG POLITICS AND THE ACT OF 1841

STATE STAY-LAWS

II

THE PERIOD OF THE DEBTOR

1827–1861

W HEN, after a ten year contest, the Bankruptcy Bill was decisively defeated in Congress in 1827, Judge Joseph Story wrote to a friend: [1]

> The Bankrupt Bill has been lost and under circumstances which will forbid any attempt to revive it for many years. It has had much of the best talent, eloquence, and influence of the Senate to support it; but it has failed from causes not likely to be overcome in future times. It interferes with State pride and prejudice, with the interests of some, with the political expectations of others, with the Antifederalism of others, and above all with that mass of public opinion which in different States of the Union floats in opposite directions, even when apparently impelled by the same common cause. I have always had some confidence that a Bankrupt Law would be passed, but I now begin to believe that the power will, in the National Government, forever remain a dead letter.

Singularly enough, it was a decision of Story's Court, a month after the writing of this letter, which, more than anything else, prevented consideration of National bankruptcy legislation for nearly ten years. Hitherto, one of the chief arguments in favor of such legislation had been the belief that the Supreme Court, when the question finally arose, would supplement its opinion in *Sturges* v. *Crowninshield* holding unconstitutional any State insolvent law applicable to previous contracts, by a further decision that *all* State insolvent laws were invalid, whether applying to previous or to future contracts, and that Congress alone had power to act on the subject.[2] Five years went by, however, and the Court still had not settled the question. There were delays even then in the administration of justice. On March 3, 1824, the day after the decision of the famous Steamboat case of *Gibbons* v. *Ogden*, there had come up from Louisiana for argument in the Supreme Court, the case of *Ogden* v. *Saunders* (12 Wheaton 213), the outcome of which would decide the point. This case had been begun in the State Court in 1814, and had reached the Supreme Court in 1820. "It will present a most interesting question," said a New York newspaper in 1824, "and next to the Steamboat Cause will be of more importance to the future welfare of the State than any other which will be agitated during the present Term. . . . If Congress declines passing any bankrupt law and the States are prohibited from adopting laws for themselves, the commercial state of the country will present a spectacle not found in history. The debtor, the merchant, whose fortune has been swept away by events beyond his control, will be pursued by unrelenting creditors without cessation." [3] This noted case was argued in 1824 by Henry Clay, David B. Ogden, and Charles G. Haines, against Daniel Webster and Henry Wheaton appearing in opposition to the validity of the State law.

The Court, being greatly divided in opinion, adjourned without rendering a decision.[4] In 1825 and 1826, owing to the illness and death of Justice Todd and the failure to appoint his successor, the Court was evenly divided, so that it was not until January, 1827, that the case was re-argued. Twelve days after the conclusion of the debate in Congress and the final defeat of the 1827 Bankruptcy Bill, the Supreme Court, on February 18, 1827, handed down a four to three decision which upheld the power of the State to pass insolvent laws as to future contracts (Chief Justice Marshall, and Justices Story and Duval dissenting), and thus set the point finally at rest, but only after eight years of doubt and litigation.[5]

This decision, of course, strengthened the position of the opponents of a National Bankrupt Law and confirmed their belief that the State insolvent laws were sufficient to deal with the relations of creditor and debtor, and that there was no need of an exertion of National power.[6] Moreover, the condition of debtors was at this time being further temporarily relieved by the passage of stay-laws and appraisal-laws in many of the newer States (of which I treat more fully *infra*); and as a writer of the period pointed out, "these statutes are, in operation, a sort of insolvent law, which though acting as a fraud in case of solvent debtors, enabled other debtors to gradually make payment." "Until these statutes have been declared unconstitutional by some competent tribunal," he said, "their operation is the same as if their validity were unimpeachable. And new statutes can be passed much faster than the old ones can be declared unconstitutional; for it is not to be supposed that the existing statutory provisions exhaust all the devices which can be used to elude the grasp of the Constitution."[7]

The condition of debtors was also being ameliorated by the spread of laws abolishing imprisonment for debt. The first of these laws was passed in Kentucky in 1821, followed by New York in 1831; Vermont, Ohio, and Michigan in 1838; Alabama in 1839; New Hampshire and Tennessee in 1840; Pennsylvania and Connecticut in 1842. In 1839, the United States abolished imprisonment for debt of all persons in Federal Courts in States which had so acted. In 1834, Maine, New Hampshire, Massachusetts, and South Carolina abolished imprisonment of debtors owing less than $5 to $30; and by 1857, when Massachusetts provided that "imprisonment for debt except in cases of fraud is hereby abolished forever," practically all the States had acted.[8] The Supreme Court in 1827 and 1838 had held such laws constitutional.[9]

It was the great Panic of 1837 and the depression of the succeeding years that revived the pressure for a bankrupt law; and this panic was primarily the result of a wild period similar to the years prior to 1929. "Everybody is speculating," wrote Michael Chevalier, the French economist, "and everything has become an object of speculation. The most daring enterprises find encouragement; all projects find subscribers. The principal objects of speculation are . . . cotton, land, city and town lots, banks, and railroads." [10] "All the world is going mad after timber land, Canton stock, South Cove Company, and like speculations which are taking the place of the lottery mania that used to possess the community," said a Baltimore newspaper, stating further that stock speculation had "become so extravagant that the Board of Brokers' room was not large enough for their accommodation." [11] Shopkeepers, small tradesmen, factory hands, farmers, lawyers, students mingled with speculators to try their fortune.[12] "A sort of mania had seized upon our community," said Nathaniel P. Tallmadge of New York in the Senate, "and by a course of untoward adventures and speculations had involved in one common deluge of disaster the fortunes of the rich and the hard earnings of the industrious. . . . There was improvident, wild, and unwarrantable abuse of individual credit."[13] The rage for gambling in land was virulent everywhere — "Michigan fever," as it was called (just as, one hundred years later, there was a "Florida fever"). Real estate of any kind could be sold at any price — swamp, farm, timber, wild, desert lands; paper cities and towns were laid out in the wilderness, everywhere, around the Great Lakes and the rivers of the West, and lots were sold at prices that could not have been realized in New York or Philadelphia even in conservative times. The city of Chicago was a product and the greatest boom town of that period, growing from 550 inhabitants in 1830 to over 5,000 in 1836; and Chicago historians have stated that: "The people chased every bubble that floated on the speculative atmosphere. The more absurd the project, the more madly was it pursued. The Government land office in the city was besieged from morning till night with eager speculators." [14]

In addition to the private speculation in land, the Western States loaded themselves with debt incurred for railroads, canals, and other public improvements that could hardly have been self supporting in old settled communities. The Federal Government policies also aggravated the situation. Sales of public lands increased from 2,777,857 acres with receipts of $3,557,024 in 1831 to 20,074,871 acres with a value of $25,167,133 in 1836. The land was paid for in State bank notes, often depreciated or irredeemable; and banks were organized in many cases by land speculators who issued notes, borrowed the notes, and bought the Government land. The notes received for sales of land were deposited by the Government in the banks, increasing their assets ($41,500,00 being on deposit in 1836) and were then borrowed again for new purchases of land.[15] Under these circumstances, the number of banks increased from 330 in 1830 to 788 at the end of 1836; banking capital increased from $110,000,000 to $378,000,000; banking loans increased from $200,000,000 to $457,000,000 and note issues from $49,000,000 to $149,000,000.[16] As this inflation of the currency went on, labor, fuel, food, rent, and interest rose to unheard of figures. The Government meanwhile had been rolling up a surplus in the Treasury and had deposited with the States $28,000,000 of it as loans.

In the midst of these conditions came severe money contraction in Europe, the specie circular of 1836 requiring all payment to the Government to be made in gold or silver, widespread failures of banks, and defalcations by private and public officials.[17] In 1837, business crashed on all sides; and three years later John C. Calhoun said in the Senate: "We are in the midst of a period of almost unexampled contraction following one remarkable above all others for the extent and duration of the expansion, for the universality and boldness of speculation and the extent and severity of the embarrassment which has followed."[18] "The country," said James J. Roosevelt in the House, "is covered with debt, contracted when currency was worth not more than half its values, when banknotes were plenty as the leaves in autumn. To exact payment now is in truth to exact two dollars for one."[19] And Daniel Webster, in a speech in Detroit in 1837, uttered these words which might almost have been uttered this last year:

In times like these, we find ourselves in the midst of a serious financial and industrial crisis. It just seems inconceivable that conditions can ever right themselves enough to have prosperous times in this country again. Trade and industry throughout the land are disorganized. Banks by the hundreds have failed. Securities have fallen to one half or even one quarter of their former values. The problem of unemployment has become general, and in all large cities special committees have been organized to provide food and clothing for the poor and unemployed. In addition to this effort, some cities have caused relief work to be instigated by public bodies. Widespread want and

55

distress have led to labor strikes. The lessening demand for wheat exported to Europe has caused American wheat to sell in the West for less than fifty cents a bushel. Extensive competition, lowering prices, and unwise speculation have brought about a crisis. . . . The renewal of confidence and the allaying of violent fear in the minds of the people which will allow for active buying rather than money hoarding must precede business recovery.

About the same time, Justice Story wrote to Justice McLean (May 10, 1837):

The old constitutional doctrines are fast fading away, and a change has come over the public mind, from which I augur little good. . . . Our country is in a state of unexampled distress and suffering. Credit and confidence and business are everywhere at a stand. . . . Will the people awake to their rights and duties? I fear not. They have become stupefied and are led on to their ruin by the arts of demagogues and the corrupted influences of party.

And at the same time, Ralph Waldo Emerson was writing in his Journal (May 31, 1837):

I see a good in such emphatic and universal calamity as the times bring. That they dissatisfy me with Society. . . . Society has played out its last stake; it is checkmated. Young men have no hope. Adults stand like day-laborers idle in the streets. None calleth us to labor. . . . The present generation is bankrupt of principles and hope, as of property.

Confronting this frightful economic situation, President Van Buren made the first official suggestion for bankruptcy legislation, in his Special Message of September 4, 1837, in which he urged a bankruptcy bill confined to banks. This, he contended, would be the most effective way of dealing with banks which failed to redeem their notes, and would afford the only practical method for relief to unfortunate note-holders. The President's suggestion met with strong opposition from five sources — first, from those who believed that the Government should not attempt to deal at all with the economic situation; second, from those who believed that a bankruptcy law applicable to corporations would be unconstitutional; third, from those who believed that the Government should not interfere with State institutions; fourth, from those who believed that the currency question ought not to be dealt with under the Bankruptcy Power; and fifth, from those who, as Whigs, bitterly opposed it as a partisan and political measure. The President's message was debated in the fall of 1837 in the Senate, without any action being taken.[20] Ten years before, a proposal to amend the Bankrupt Bill, in 1827, so as to include corporations had been rejected. Daniel Webster now voiced strong opposition, saying that it would be "a great perversion of the power conferred upon Congress to exercise it upon corporations and bankers, with the leading or primary object of remedying a depreciated paper currency"; also that no bankruptcy law could be defended as uniform which applied only to bankers. Other Whigs like John J. Crittenden and Robert Strange of North Carolina also argued against the constitutionality of such a measure. John C. Calhoun voiced views which anticipated those of many conservatives of today:

BANKRUPTCY IN UNITED STATES HISTORY

After the best reflection I am of the impression that Government can do little in the way of relief, and that it is a case which must be mainly left to the constitution of the patient. . . . I dread the doctor and his drugs more than the disease itself. The distress of the country consists in its indebtedness and can only be relieved by the payment of its debts. To effect this, industry, frugality, economy, and time are necessary. I rely more on the growing crops — on the cotton, rice and tobacco of the South — than on all the projects or devices of politicians. I am opposed to all coercion by this Government. . . . We have arrived at a remarkable era in our political history. The days of legislative and executive encroachment, of tariffs and surpluses, of bank and public debt and extravagant expenditure, are past for the present. . . . We are about to take a fresh start. I move off under the State rights banner and go in the direction in which I have been so long moving. I seize the opportunity thoroughly to reform the Government, to bring it back to its original principles, to retrench and economize and rigidly to enforce accountability. I shall oppose strenuously all attempts to originate a new debt, to create a national bank, to reunite the political and money power (more dangerous than that of church and State), in any form or shape . . . and mainly I shall use my best efforts to give an ascendency to the great conservative principle of State sovereignty over the dangerous and despotic doctrine of consolidation.

The arguments by the Whigs and by many Southern Democrats were replied to by strong Democrats like Silas Wright of New York, John M. Niles of Connecticut, and especially by Thomas H. Benton of Missouri. A broken bank, said the latter, was appropriately, primarily, and peculiarly the subject of a bankruptcy bill, which "the English and other

58

moderns have diverted to humbler games." And, said he, there was nothing to prevent Mr. Webster or anyone else moving to include in a bankrupt bill other classes than bankers; but, he added, "Webster, true to the habits of the legal profession which have become a proverbial disqualification for the proper exercise of legislative duties . . . runs to English law books. Legislators should consider the difference between the political institutions of the two countries, and transfer our contemplation to *actual* bankruptcy among ourselves, rather than to *historical* bankruptcy in England." The necessity of a curb upon the banks "which have become an element of political power and the basis of a moneyed aristocracy" was urged by Niles. "On the one side," he said, "the popular will, the great mass of the people; on the other are the banks and the moneyed power. On the one side is the aristocracy of wealth; on the other the democracy of numbers. The struggle will be arduous and probably long; but the result cannot be doubtful." To this, Oliver H. Smith of Indiana said "that for his part, he did not know where this aristocracy was. They knew no distinctions in the West. . . . He protested against that spirit of uncharitableness which would array one class against another. We could never advance the interests of the nation by inciting one portion of the people to envy another." Nothing resulted from this debate; and during the next two years (1838 and 1839) of Van Buren's Administration, owing to the struggle over his financial policy, no effort was made to revive bankruptcy for banks. But a renewal of the financial crisis in 1839, through the crashing of many more banks and prolongation of the depression, revived the demand for relief by a National bankruptcy law; and in 1840 and 1841, debates over bills on this subject occurred in the 26th Congress, during which there appeared a new approach to the subject.[21] No longer was it regarded merely from the creditors' point of view. The debtors were now making their influence strongly felt. For the first time in history, a bill (in 13 sections) was introduced (by Daniel Webster) which provided for voluntary bankruptcy for "all persons whatsoever owing debts," and for compulsory or involuntary bankruptcy for traders only. When this bill was reported out by the Judiciary Committee, the debtor class had gained a complete victory, for the bill (to be in force for two years) provided for voluntary bankruptcy *only*. At once, Garrett D. Wall of New Jersey proposed a substitute bill (of 17 sections) to include both voluntary and compulsory bankruptcy, the latter being confined to traders (including corporations). "The idea of a bankrupt law designed and framed for the exclusive benefit of the bankrupt," he said, "originated in the Chamber of the Judiciary Committee. . . . No precedent of such a bill is to be found. . . . It creates a general jubilee for debtors, it is an insolvent law in its inception . . . a novel, untried experiment which would prove a curse instead of a blessing to the honest bankrupt. . . . It is liable to radical and fundamental objections, apart from its unconstitution-

THE PERIOD OF THE DEBTOR

ality. . . . It holds out a temptation to every debtor to push his speculations to the brink of rashness and recklessness, by affording him a sure refuge in case of wreck, at the sole hazard of the creditor." He contended that the word "uniform" in the Constitution meant not "territorially or locally but as to the classes and subject matter upon which the bankrupt bill should pass." This was a leading argument for half a century against the various proposals for bankruptcy legislation, until the Supreme Court decided that uniformity meant geographical uniformity. Wall admitted that his own bill by including a voluntary feature was new, but that it was appropriate "to the progress and expansion of the credit system, the purposes of trade, and the spirit of the age." A furious debate took place for over two months, and again the attack on the bill united many divergent elements.

Many Democrats opposed any National bankruptcy bill whatever; and James Buchanan, in particular, urged that such a measure was inapplicable to the conditions in this country, that the great distance to the Federal Courts would make them exceedingly oppressive. Many other Democrats and many Whigs opposed voluntary bankruptcy as unconstitutional. John C. Calhoun said that the bill was not a law on the subject of bankruptcy at all, but was a pure insolvent law, and that the terms "were not convertible, as the Convention of 1787 well knew." He deplored "the loose and unsafe construction of the Constitution, which arises out of

61

present distress and sympathy." Thomas H. Benton also opposed the voluntary bill as unconstitutional — a bill "merely for the abolition of existing debts under the mock name of a system of bankruptcy — a mere insolvent law at the will of the debtor." And, said he, "it will teach the rising generation a facile way to get rid of their obligations after squandering the money and property which they had obtained upon the faith of paying for it." Henry Hubbard of New Hampshire said that the Constitution would never have been ratified if this power had been believed to exist, and that if Congress could extend a voluntary bill to farmers, it could extend a compulsory one. He also opposed the voluntary feature as only "admirably calculated in favor of dishonest debtors and rogues." Wilson Lumpkin of Georgia also not only doubted the constitutionality of the bill, but believed that the policy of such a bill was wrong and odious. "Honesty is not only the best policy, but it is a moral duty," he said. "We should advise the people to work more and spend less; to pay their old debts and be cautious how they contract new ones. . . . The only true basis of credit is industry, economy, punctuality, and honesty." Alexander Anderson of Tennessee said that the bill, "as a great statute sponge," would be "a heavy blow to the moral feeling of society," and would "strike down the main pillar of credit, which is confidence inspired by integrity and justice." Silas Wright believed that the bill would not be "uniform" unless it included both voluntary and involuntary bankruptcy, but believed that voluntary bankrupts should not be discharged unless fifty per cent of their creditors assented. (A motion to this effect was lost, 20 to 22.)

On the other hand, the voluntary feature was the only thing which made the bill acceptable to most of the Whigs and to some Northern Democrats; and many were entirely opposed to the compulsory section. Foremost of the advocates of voluntary bankruptcy alone, was Henry Clay. In moving to strike out the compulsory section, he said that this very section was only "a substantial copy from the insolvent system of one of the States [Massachusetts]. There is, therefore, no necessity for Federal legislation in behalf of the creditors." "Compulsory bankruptcy is not called for by the voice of the people, either the rich or the poor," said Nathan F. Dixon of Rhode Island. "Nor is it required for the protection of the creditor; he has his remedy for collection of debts, cheaper and more summary, in the State laws. . . . A compulsory law might bring to ruin many now on the brink who otherwise will recover." Urging, however, that a voluntary law, if passed, should not be "a temporary relief law, a mere sponge to wipe out the old scores of the present insolvent debtors," he moved to strike out the two year limitation, which was defeated by a vote of 13 to 32.[22] He argued forcibly that the Bankruptcy Power extended beyond traders and could apply to all voluntary petitioners:

Jealousy at exercise of the power originates in the mistaken analogies between English laws and those which Congress are authorized to enact. This appeared in the

Federal Convention. The limited intercourse between the
States in the early years was calculated to foster local feelings and views and natural suggestions of State jealousy
that the exercise of this power (however desirable in some
States and especially with those the most commercial)
might be prejudicial to others. Besides, the country was
rather agricultural than commercial in its pursuits, bearing
relations of life not the most likely to awaken strong and
active sympathies in favor of the insolvent debtor. This
consideration naturally secured a preference for State
insolvent laws corresponding better, as might be thought,
with the local concerns of the day. But the relations of
business in this country are greatly changed and enlarged.
The modern facilities of intercourse have brought all the
States together in a common market. The North and
South are in the constant interchange of their products
and merchandise. This is calculated to give national uniformity to the rules of trade and induces the necessity
of uniformity in the treatment of the relation of debtor
and creditor.

Clay's motion, however, to strike out the compulsory section, though supported by Webster and most
of the Whigs, was defeated by a vote of 17 to 25.

The strongest opposition to the whole measure
came from Thomas H. Benton of Missouri, who
would not accept any bankruptcy bill which did not
apply to corporations. "Their wealth, their number,
their privileges, duties, conduct, their relation to the
community — all made them pre-eminently fit and
proper subjects for the application of a bankruptcy
law." There were nearly 1,000 banking corporations,
"an oligarchy" which had filled the country with un-
redeemed paper, and the whole Union was filled with

other corporations engaged in every conceivable pursuit. "Associated wealth," he said, "is now the order of the day, chartered incorporations possess an immense proportion of the wealth of the country. The privileges of corporations are also very great. They are too strong for individuals to contend with and therefore should be placed in contention with a strong power. They are too strong for State power and therefore should be placed in contention with the power of the United States." Franklin Pierce of New Hampshire and Robert J. Walker of Mississippi believed that the inclusion of corporations was "the most important, if not the redeeming provision of the bill." On the other hand, Cassius C. Clay of Alabama opposed the proposal to include banking corporations as an interference with State Rights (many States including Alabama being stockholders in banks). John J. Clayton of Delaware said that control over corporations in bankruptcy was an alarming and tremendous power for Congress to exercise, never within the contemplation of the framers of the Constitution. He charged that it was a Democratic policy intended to destroy the banks. "The fanaticism of party," he said, "was very like fanaticism in religion, always ready to go to extremes to accomplish its objects and reckless of consequences." And he pointed out that, for a Democratic and Southern measure, it interfered alarmingly with the rights and control of the States over corporations, as a lever which would extend to any length to uproot every corporation in the country. And he added:

I have never been the noisy champion of State Rights ... but if there be any politician here of that school who is willing to vote for this amendment, he has a stronger stomach and greater powers of digestion than I suppose one to have. But are these political dogmas really entertained or not? Heaven knows that I sometimes doubt and think they are used only as tubs thrown out to amuse the great Southern whale.

Oliver H. Smith of Indiana also opposed this "most alarming and tremendous extension of Federal powers, which will swallow up and engulph within their tremendous vortex, every vestige of State rights and change the entire nature of the Government. The power of creating corporations is one of the highest attributes of sovereignty. . . . The State banks being the creatures of the State and possessing a portion of the sovereignty must in the very nature of things be subject alone to the control of the Government that created them. . . . A power in the States to erect corporations and a power in the Federal Government to pull them down cannot exist at the same time."

In spite of all the above, Thomas H. Benton said that the "inclusion of corporations is the hinge on which the passage of any law will depend." The attitude of the Democrats on this issue was only another example of the fact, so often illustrated in our history, that the dogma of State Rights is conveniently reversible, and that it has been a party doctrine only when its application would suit the party. In fact, it has generally meant only State Rights for the right

States. Even those Democrats who opposed inclusion of banks did so, in fact, less on the State Rights' doctrine, than in the belief that it would ruin the weak Southern banks and put the strong Northern banks in control.[23] Clay's motion to eliminate banks was carried, however, by a vote of 28 to 10, with Webster and the Whigs and Calhoun and the State Rights' Democrats voting together.

The ablest argument for the bill was made by Daniel Webster; and it was chiefly through his power and eloquence that the measure was carried.[24] He favored a bill providing for both voluntary and involuntary bankruptcy, but said that, as there were many objections to the latter, especially from the Western States, he was content with what he could get, even voluntary bankruptcy alone, as he considered a relief law now absolutely necessary. And he said:

I am free to confess my leading object to be to relieve those who are at present bankrupt, hopeless bankrupts, and who cannot be discharged or set free but by a bankrupt act passed by Congress. . . . It is this case which has created the general cry for this measure. . . . I believe the interest of creditors would be greatly benefitted even by a system of voluntary bankruptcy alone, and I am quite confident that the public good would be eminently promoted. . . . I verily believe that the power of perpetuating debts against debtors, for no substantial good to the creditor himself, and the power of imprisonment for debt, at least as it existed in this country ten years ago, have imposed more restraint on personal liberty than the law of debtor and creditor imposes in any other Christian and commercial country. (To my knowledge, there are many who cannot come here to the seat of Government for fear of arrest by creditors in some intervening State or in the District of Columbia.)

Of the constitutionality both of voluntary bankruptcy alone and of inclusion of other classes than traders, he had no doubt. He quoted Judge Story's view that, in general (Sections 1106–1113), "a law on the subject of bankruptcies in the sense of the Constitution is a law making provision for cases of persons failing to pay their debts." [25] He opposed application of the law to banks, though he admitted that the people of Massachusetts had a "pretty strong disposition in favor of the proposal, as they are among the greatest sufferers by the present ruinous state of things." [26] In view of the intense opposition to the application of the law to corporations, it is interesting to note that Judge Story wrote to Webster (who had consulted with him) that he saw no "absolutely insuperable objections" to the proposal, though "there are some practical difficulties"; but, he added, with a tenderness for State Rights unusual with him: "Is it quite certain that State Rights as to the creation and dissolution of corporations are not thus virtually infringed? I confess that I feel no small doubt whether Congress can regulate State corporations by any other laws than State law." [27]

At the end of this two months' debate, the bill carrying both voluntary and involuntary bankruptcy, but without application to corporations, finally passed the Senate on June 25, 1840, by the close vote of 21 to 19. The division was practically on geographical lines — the North and East against the South and part of the West. It was characterized rightly and prophetically by Alexander O. Anderson of Tennessee as "the most singular compromise ever presented in legislative history. It is no more or less than that the voluntary bankrupt is to be allowed to escape from his creditors upon condition that creditors may be allowed to oppress a particular class of debtors. . . . This bill," said he, "will array the North against the South, and will engender a suspicion, a distrust, a deep rooted prejudice which can scarcely be obliterated during the quarter of a century." As this was the last year of Van Buren's Administration, there was no likelihood of its passage by the House, then in Democratic control; and Congress adjourned July 21, 1840, without giving any relief to the unfortunate debtors of the country. The depression had then lasted three years.

Before the next Congress met, the Presidential campaign was fought and won by the Whigs; and in it the bankruptcy bill was made one of their party issues. In fact, their opponents claimed that the political influence of the 400,000 bankrupts in the country may have turned the scale in five States having 89 electoral votes, in which there were 900,000 voters and in which there was only a Whig majority of 18,000 votes — among these States being New York, Maine, and Pennsylvania.[28]

At the first and extra session of the 27th Congress, President Tyler, on June 30, 1841, sent a Message to the House transmitting a memorial signed by 3,000 citizens of New York, praying for a bankruptcy law. "This process of petitioning Congress through the President is a novelty," said John Quincy Adams.[29] In addition, memorials were presented from the Legislatures of six States in which there had been great debtor distress — Maine, Massachusetts, New York, Louisiana, Mississippi and Michigan. In his Message, the President said:

> That a bankrupt law, carefully guarded against fraudulent practices and embracing as far as practicable all classes of society — the failure to do which has heretofore constituted a prominent objection to the measure — would afford extreme relief I do not doubt. The distress incident to the derangements of some years past has visited large numbers of our fellow citizens with hopeless insolvency, whose energies both mental and physical, by reason of the load of debt pressing upon them, are lost to the country. Whether Congress shall deem it proper to enter upon the consideration of the subject at its present extraordinary session it will doubtless wisely determine. I have fulfilled my duty to the memorialists in submitting their petition to your consideration.

John McPherson Berrien of Georgia had already introduced in the Senate the same bankruptcy bill which had passed at the previous session and which was a skillfully written statute, principally drafted by Daniel Webster and Judge Story, and modelled on the highly successful insolvency law of Massachusetts of 1838.[30] Unlike previous bills, this was now made a strict Whig party measure.[31] As soon as it was reported, the Democrats moved to amend it by making it applicable to banking corporations; and Thomas H. Benton, Levi Woodbury, Robert J. Walker, and other Democratic leaders argued for this amendment, without which, they said, no bill could pass.[32] Nathaniel P. Tallmadge of New York deplored the "paltry considerations of party" and said that the friends of the bill at the last session had endeavored to divest it altogether of a party character. He expressed his painful regret at reading in the *Washington Globe* an unjust aspersion on Clay. The *Globe* had said that if the bill's friends would join the Democrats and put the banks in the bill, it might be passed "without the license of Mr. Clay, but it is not in Mr. Clay's programme and that omission is a death warrant to it. It is good political capital for the next Presidential election and was worth 500,000 votes at the last." The warm friends of the measure were against "the fatal delusion" of the suggestion as to inclusion of banks, said Tallmadge. "At the last session, it was struck out on motion of opponents of the bill and they then voted against the bill itself. No bill can become a law that includes banks." Ambrose H. Sevier of Arkansas, Clement C. Clay of Alabama, John Henderson of Mississippi, and John McPherson Berrien of Georgia opposed the amendment as "an invasion of sovereignty of the States of which the corporations were but emanations." The bank amendment, as added to by Richard H. Bayard of Delaware, so as to include State-owned banking corporations, was finally defeated by a vote of 16 to 34 (all those voting aye being Democrats). Thereupon, John C. Calhoun renewed his attack on the bill

71

as unconstitutional, because of its voluntary bankruptcy section, and because of its retrospective action.
Benton agreed with Calhoun as to the invalidity of
the measure. Lewis F. Linn of Missouri also opposed
any except a prospective law. James Buchanan vigorously attacked it as a bill simply "to rub out and begin
again. . . . The facility with which debtors could
wipe out their obligations might make them less careful in the contract of debts in the future. The be-
setting sin of this country is a universal love of
money, a disposition to speculate and grow rich in a
day, instead of by long and patient industry."
"And," said he, "the rein is needed in this case, and
not the spur." He believed the number of bankrupts
in the country had been greatly exaggerated. There
were only 30,000,000 voters. Were one-sixth or one-
seventh bankrupt, he asked? He would venture to
predict that before two years expired the bill would be
repealed.

The bill passed on July 25, 1841, after a three days'
debate, by a vote of 26 to 23 — the division being
almost wholly on party lines.

In the House, there was great opposition, based on
diverse grounds. The Northern Whigs opposed inclusion of banks. Some Democrats believed the voluntary section unconstitutional. Some Whigs objected to the very limited provisions as to compulsory
bankruptcy. "Apparently that part of the bill is
only a ship to carry the voluntary bankruptcy sections," said Joseph Trumbull of Connecticut. "Voluntary bankruptcy is a new term. Who ever heard

such language before? Under this bill, discharge of debtor is the thing principally aimed at. Under previous acts, surrender of property was the chief object." On the other hand, James C. Sprigg of Kentucky said that "the bankrupt law seemed designed not to give relief to the debtor but to give a more efficient remedy to the creditor and he would not let his Yankee friends in New York and Massachusetts which still tolerated imprisonment for debt legislate for Kentucky." He referred to the fact that Kentucky in 1821 had passed relief laws "in times of unparalleled distress — laws not to violate contracts or to relieve the debtor from his debts, but merely to suspend compulsory proceedings for two years; and yet the merchants of the Atlantic States endeavored by aid of the Federal Courts to set aside these laws and subject the citizens of Kentucky to imprisonment." Others objected to forcing creditors into Federal Courts at all; believed that the Government had no power to discharge prior contracts; and thought that a bankrupt system could only be applied to commercial traders. "A bankruptcy bill," said Henry A. Wise of Virginia, "is not suited to the business and habits of an agricultural people. Its provisions are incompatible with the interests of the corn, tobacco and cotton planters. . . . This bill is a political measure. It is said there are 500,000 bankrupts, but," he asked, "how many creditors? Five at least to each debtor — hence there will be 2,500,000 for repeal." John Pope of Kentucky said the bill should be entitled "an Act for the benefit of lawyers, clerks, etc." Victory Birdseye of New York also said that the numbers of bankrupts had been largely exaggerated; and of the 45,000 petitioners for the bill, many signed on lithographic blanks, "copies from the same block whether those from New York or from Illinois." He warned his party against this novelty in legislation. "The ship, I suppose, will be called 'Experiment' as it is to be another experiment upon the business of the people. And will not a Whig Congress be warned, by the fate of those who have gone before them, that experiments by Government upon the business of the people and bringing vexations and disappointment into their affairs are arguments which tell with effect upon the popular mind?"

The ablest defense of the bill was made by William P. Fessenden of Maine. To the constitutional objections raised, he said:

I have a word or two to say of the fondness which exists at the present time for interposing constitutional doubts and scruples upon almost every question of legislative deliberation. . . . I wish to see that Constitution what its framers designed it to be — powerful for good — effective, energetic, broad, and deep. Those who would narrow it down to the smallest possible dimensions, would, if successful, destroy its vitality. They would destroy its hold upon the admiration and love of the American people. . . . They would render that noble forest tree a dry and barren and unsightly trunk.

He stated that it was not true that the law was called for only by the debtor class, as merchants from almost every large city had petitioned for it. It was also not true that the agricultural community would not benefit by it. They were most interested. They sell more than they buy and generally to distant points. Western cattle, pork, and grain find their markets in Charleston or New Orleans. Southern producers deal with Northern traders. Under the present insolvency laws, distant and foreign creditors, unable to be on the watch, get nothing; and local creditors in the North benefit by preference and attachment laws. And on the general proposition of the necessity of the possession of power by the National Government to relieve men from pressure of debts, he said:

The power of Government to pass laws affecting the obligation of contracts is derived from the nature of the Government itself. . . . It is a necessary power, for it is by no means difficult to imagine a condition of things in which the safety and well being of the State would imperatively demand its exercise. Take the case, for example, in which a whole community becomes insolvent by some stupendous accident, or by some magnificent but fallacious scheme, such as other countries have seen and felt at no distant day. Can it be pretended that a power to apply a remedy to a disorder that is paralyzing and destroying the body politic exists nowhere? Such an idea is a libel upon the very name of Government. And yet if we have not this power, it exists nowhere in this country. It is yielded up by the States. . . . I am willing to concede that the Government of the United States is peculiar, that it possesses no power not granted expressly or by necessary implication. In this respect, it differs from all others, and, so far, my argument arising from the general nature of government does not apply. But the existence of the principle

75

when taken in connection with the express grant of power on the one hand and the exclusion of it on the other, together with the necessity of its being found somewhere, render my conclusion clearly unavoidable. . . . It is true, indeed, that a power like this should be most cautiously exercised. As a general rule, the obligation of contracts should be held inviolable. Regard should always be had to the interests and rights of the citizens. But those rights and those interests must yield to high considerations of public policy. They must necessarily be made subservient to the good of the State. I grant that no sympathy for human suffering, no desire to benefit individuals or classes of individuals, can alone demand its exercise. Legislation of this kind must be founded upon higher views and more commanding principles — principles which look to the common weal — to national objects. Whenever these are brought into action, they necessarily ride over all those considerations which affect individuals merely, and become imperative upon every statesman whose eye is single to the welfare of the whole country.

Eugenius A. Nisbett of Georgia made also a strong argument as to the benefit of such a law to the merchants of the South and West. On them, he said, the inequality in the rights of citizens of different States under the State insolvent laws is peculiarly oppressive, for they buy and sell largely in the cities of the North.

The opposition to the bill was so strong that a motion to lay it on the table, with all amendments, was carried on August 17, 1841, by the decisive vote of 110 to 97; and everyone thought the bill was finally defeated. At this point, there occurred one of the most skillful and remarkable pieces of political maneuvering in our legislative history, and perhaps one of the clearest cases of logrolling or "political bargain and sale" (as its opponents termed it).[33] The Whig programme under the leadership of Clay at this time was to put through three great measures — a bill for the distribution of Government lands and their proceeds, a bill for preservation of the protective tariff revenues, and a bill for a National Fiscal Bank and the over-riding of President Tyler's veto of it. A subsidiary of this programme was the passage of the Bankrupt Bill. No one of these measures had the same body of supporters; but each could possibly be carried by a promise of votes for the other three. Tyler's veto had arrived in the Senate on August 16, 1841, and had been greeted by hisses in the gallery.[34] On the next day (the day when the House had rejected the Bankrupt Bill), the Senate moved to lay aside the veto of the Fiscal Bank bill and take up the Distribution Bill. Meanwhile, in the House on the next morning after the Bankrupt Bill's defeat, reconsideration of the vote was moved, a call of the House was ordered, the doors and windows of the Hall were closed, the names of absentees were again called, excuses were received, and most of the absentees presented themselves at the door; whereupon, the motion to reconsider was carried by a vote of 168 to 98, and the Bankrupt Bill was taken up from the table and passed by a vote of 110 to 106 — almost exactly the reverse of the opposite vote of the previous day (110 to 97). Opponents of the bill later charged that this change was brought about by the party lash, as a part of a bargain to pass the Distribution Bill, Eastern votes being obtained for the latter bill in return for Western for the bankruptcy measure. "The bill had been laid on the table, where everyone supposed it was destined to sleep the sleep of death," said Congressman John B. Weller of Ohio. "The Whig members were entertained that evening at a certain board where the champagne flowed pretty freely, and where rumor said an agreement was made to reconsider the next morning. The next day the motion was reconsidered — the majority having determined, when the wine flowed freely the night before, to change their determination. It was found necessary to the passage of another bill — the Land Distribution Bill. . . . The whole legislation of the extra session was accomplished by contract." [35]

The House bill arrived in the Senate on August 18, in the midst of a debate on the motion to postpone consideration of the Fiscal Bank veto. Lewis F. Linn of Missouri said he understood that the Bankrupt Bill had been forced through in the House by a majority of 5 votes, while "many of its Whig opponents were dodging behind columns" to escape voting. "This is the measure," said William R. King of Alabama, "which is to hurry this Land Distribution Bill to its final passage without amendment or debate; when the Bankrupt Bill was laid on the table yesterday in the House, the Distribution Bill could not by any possibility be passed in this Senate; the Distribution Bill is the price of the Bankrupt Law; the screws have been put on. I have never seen legislation so openly and shamefully disgraced by a system of bargain and sale." Robert J. Walker of Mississippi then moved to lay the Distribution Bill on the table and to take up the bankruptcy measure, and thereupon, over the strong objections of Benton and Buchanan, the House amendments were concurred in and the bill sent back to the House, where it was received (as the Reporter states) with cries of "Good," "Bravo," "Go it." It became the Bankrupt Act of August 19, 1841 (5 Stat. 1440), the second in our history, after a lapse of thirty-eight years since the repeal of the Act of 1800. Eight days later the Distribution Bill was passed by a vote of 28 to 23.[36]

So ended, temporarily, this great struggle. John Quincy Adams wrote in his Diary: "I believe no bankrupt law can, in this country, be of much benefit to the class of creditors. The bankrupt law of 1800 operated as a receipt in full for some hundreds of men who had large debts and nothing to pay. This bill will pass some thousands through the same process. There has been for forty years since that law expired an overpowering prejudice against any bankrupt law; and now by a sudden and unaccountable revulsion, there comes a whirlwind to carry it through." [37]

Since the law, as passed, was not to take effect until February 1, 1842, a determined though unsuccessful move was made by Benton at the December, 1841, session of the Senate to postpone or to repeal it before it went into operation. He termed the measure "the impious offspring of *Bank* and *State*; he detested and abhorred it. It was an insult and outrage upon the 19th Century — big with shame and ruin to the present age and disastrous in its influence upon posterity. The rising generation must feel its baleful influence." Calhoun agreed that it was "one of the most flagrant laws ever passed Congress." [38] Henry Clay, on the other hand, said that "the Act was recommended not only by all considerations of justice, humanity, and benevolence, but no less by the appalling conditions of the country." He further stated that it was part of a system of bills for relief affecting differently the interests of different sections "which in their separate character would have been voted down because they might have been considered injurious to particular systems. Gentlemen who voted for them (he, like others) did so because it was part of a system." This was a frank admission of the logrolling character of the legislation. Benton's repeal bill was rejected, and Judge Story (who as one of the authors of the law was keenly interested) wrote: "The Bankrupt Act has had a breathing spell left for it. How long it will be suffered to live, I cannot tell. But if Congress will leave the Courts to carry it into effect, I firmly believe that it will become a most useful and salutary law. I, at least, will do all I can to give it a fair operation and a cheap one." [39] Two months later, after the law had gone into operation, Story wrote:

The Bankrupt Act works well. The Courts, at least in my Circuit, are working through all the difficulties incident to a new system. . . . I do not hesitate to say that the system is far less defective than the hasty examiner might suppose; and if Congress will let it alone for another year

80

and leave the Courts to adjust the machinery, probe the defects, and dispel some of the supposed embarassments which must show in all new systems in giving them a practical operation, I am persuaded that the system will grow popular and will be one of the most lasting benefits ever conferred upon our country.

That the bill worked well, however, and was generally successful was known from the replies to a circular inquiry sent out by Webster as Secretary of State. Most of those coming from Supreme Court and other Federal Judges testified to the law's salutary effect, though some amendments to perfect the machinery were offered.[40] Some replies from the agricultural States took a different view, based on the prevalent idea that there was a conflict between the agricultural and the commercial interest.[41] At all events, 33,739 persons took advantage of its benefits, of whom only 765 were refused discharge (with 1,468 still pending in 1862).[42] The amount of debt involved was $440,934,000, and the amount of property surrendered by the debtor $43,697,357. Owing to expenses of administration, and also owing to the fact that large numbers of the debtors had already been through the State Insolvency Courts,[43] very small dividends were paid to the creditors. One of the chief benefits which accrued from the law never showed itself in the statistics; for, as Judge Samuel L. Betts reported to Webster, there was a comparatively small number of voluntary bankrupts shown in the New York District, owing to the fact of "the very general composition of debts induced by the passage of the law."

In spite of all these facts, the law became rapidly unpopular. The creditor class saw that great crowds of debtors were being discharged from debts without any adequate payment, and that administration of the debtor's estate was very expensive and entirely in the hands of the Courts and their assignees instead of under the control of the creditors. The debtor class itself found that while the statute preserved all State liens, it had not preserved the various State exemptions of property from execution and other protective provisions furnished by the States to debtors.[44] Moreover, as Roscoe Conkling of New York said later, many felt that the Act was so incomplete as to machinery, that it could hardly be executed at all. "Indeed the Judges were driven to turn legislators and to help it out by vigorous construction and by cumbrous and interminable rules. . . . The compulsory provision never took practical effect but the voluntary provisions had full sweep." Another dangerous aspect of the law was urged by the Charleston Chamber of Commerce, which said that:

It is fraught with evils of a more dangerous character and far greater magnitude. The tremendous revulsion that took place in the currency of Great Britain in 1836, and the reverses that followed in this country, both in the monetary and commercial classes, among corporations and individuals have continued in successive shocks to the present time. . . . Cotton has reduced in value fifty per cent, and property of every description in like ratio; and securities that were supposed to be of the most solid character and known from the experience of years to be of the most ready convertibility have either lost their entire value or become wholly inconvertible. In this state of unparalleled depression, the least propitious for enforcing the collection of debts or the sale of property, it is proposed under this law to bring into immediate liquidation, under the orders of the Court, the affairs of all the insolvent debtors of the country.

It pointed out the probable immense sacrifices of property which would be avoided if left to gradual liquidation and to "the wise and humane compromises of a people naturally sagacious." And it further stated that "banks and other corporations are exempted from the Act and may throw the merchant into the Bankruptcy Court, while their own affairs are in a state of insolvency, and that, too, after aiding to ruin the merchant by the depression of an unredeemable currency." [45]

On top of all these causes for dissatisfaction, the political effects of the Act had been extremely disappointing to the Whigs. As was said in the House by a Democratic opponent: "The Whigs feared in 1841 that if they did not pass the bankrupt law they would lose New York and Maine, but they had not been paid the consideration." "A killing frost has occurred in Ohio, Pennsylvania, New York, Maine and Maryland and the verdict is against the Whigs. Clay has fallen like Wolsey," said another Democrat. And Wise of Virginia said sarcastically that "the Whigs had passed the bill to get the votes of 500,000 bankrupt debtors, and now that these debtors did not exist, they were considering the 500,000 creditors." There were also some Whigs in Congress who believed that the object of the law had been accomplished, and who had only voted for it "to relieve the existing sufferers from enduring miseries brought upon them by rash and wicked measures of financial quacks and political gamblers — growing out of twelve years of misrule, and thrown into insolvency by the maladministration of public affairs." [46]

Under the above circumstances, the Senate of the third session of the 27th Congress witnessed the curious sight of the Whig leader who introduced the Act in the first session supporting the bill for its repeal introduced by Thomas H. Benton, the Act's most bitter opponent.[47] This statute, said Benton, has proved to be nothing but a great insolvent law for the abolition of debts. "It has expunged the State insolvent laws and has met the universal condemnation of the country." He still insisted on its unconstitutionality. "The attempt to confound insolvency and bankruptcy and to make Congress supreme over both was the most daring attack on the Constitution, on the State laws, on the rights of property, and on public morals which the history of Europe or America exhibited." He called on the people and the Courts so to brand it as invalid and to hold all debtors discharged under it as uncertified bankrupts. "Congress must be driven back within the pale of the Constitution. . . . Congress has no inherent or supreme authority over debts. It cannot abolish debts as it pleases. The attempt to do so is despotism, such as can only be looked for in a Government which has no limit either in its moral or political powers. A law providing for repudiation at the will of the debtor is subversive of civil society." William Allen of Ohio said that the bill was "condemned by the undivided voice of the country," and Jabez W. Huntington of Connecticut said that he "was persuaded that the great mass of his constituents had entirely changed their opinions." Woodbury and Buchanan repeated their former opposition and prophecies of failure of the law.

On the other side, Berrien of Georgia admitted that public opinion was against the law, or rather, adverse to the voluntary feature rather than to a system of mercantile bankruptcy; and accordingly, he favored an amendment to convert the Act into a permanent commercial bankruptcy law. He denied, however, that the frauds and evils predicted had resulted. The Senate would not listen to Berrien's plea; it voted for total repeal by a vote of 32 to 13; and the House passed the repeal by a vote of 140 to 71 — members of both parties uniting to form the heavy majorities. And so the second National Bankrupt Act went out of existence, having lasted only a little over one year.

One circumstance, in connection with this Act of 1841, should be particularly noticed as having a bearing on legislation of the present day. It is this — that though the constitutionality of the Act had been long and violently attacked, the Act was passed, achieved its purpose of discharging thousands of debtors, and was repealed, before any decision as to its constitutionality was made by the Supreme Court. In other words, it had done its work and disappeared, before the question of its validity was decided by the Court. This phase of the working of our judicial system under the Constitution is frequently overlooked by law writers and historians — the fact that a Federal statute may be operative and fulfill its function completely, before reaching a final test in the Supreme Court. As a notable example, take the Reconstruction legislation. This field is worthy of exploration by legal scholars. In the case of the Act of 1841, the effect came about as follows.

In September, 1842 (prior to repeal of the Act), Judge Wells, in the United States District Court in Missouri in the case of *In re Klein*, held the Act unconstitutional and dismissed 900 cases pending in his Court (only two of which were involuntary petitions).[48] Shortly after this, a like view of the Act was held by United States District Judge in Kentucky, who adjourned a case into the Circuit Court, where the Judges, being opposed in opinion, certified the question of the validity of the Act to the Supreme Court. The latter Court in 1843 (after the repeal of the Act) dismissed the case for lack of jurisdiction.[49] Justice Catron, however, filed a strong dissenting opinion on the merits and upheld the validity of the law, and later in the Circuit on an appeal of the *Klein Case* reversed Judge Wells' decision. After that, it is a singular fact that the Supreme Court itself never passed directly upon the question of the Act's constitutionality in any case. Between 1843 and 1848, however, it decided four cases involving questions of statutory construction under the Act; so that in the great case of *Houston* v. *City Bank of New Orleans* in 1848, Reverdy Johnson and Henry Clay in argument contended that the Court had already affirmed the power of Congress "by decree under it," and had "decided the constitutionality of the law by acting under it." But neither in that case, nor in any of the thirteen other cases decided under the Act of 1841 from 1848 to 1865, did the Court specifically consider the constitutional question.[50] Yet before the next bankruptcy law was enacted after the Civil War (in 1867) everyone, lawyers and Courts alike, had so thoroughly accepted the principle of voluntary bankruptcy as being within the Constitutional power of Congress, that the question was not even raised, when the Act of 1867 was being debated. That which was of doubtful constitutionality in 1841 had become unquestioned law in 1867 — and without any specific decision by the Supreme Court.

For the next fifteen years from the date of the repeal of the Act of 1841, not only was the question of the constitutionality of voluntary bankruptcy not seriously raised, but there was practically no agitation either for or against any National bankruptcy law. The chief reason for this was that it was a period of prosperity. There was, however, one reason why the lack of such a law during this period was not more seriously felt, namely, the fact that in the decade following the Panic of 1837 many States had passed stay-laws and appraisal-laws for the protection of debtors, forbidding sale on execution or foreclosure unless the property should be sold for one half, or two thirds, of its appraised value. Such laws were enacted in 1836 by Pennsylvania; in 1837 by Virginia; in 1840 by Mississippi; in 1841 by Ohio, Illinois, and Indiana (renewing a stay-law repealed in 1838); in 1842 by Virginia and by Pennsylvania; in 1843 by Iowa. Laws were also passed extending the time for redemption of mortgages by Alabama, Minnesota, Michigan, New York, and other States. In addition, the States began to exempt more and more of a debtor's property from execution, as shown by laws of Georgia, Kentucky, Tennessee, Michigan, Missouri, and New York in 1842. Texas in 1846 went so far as to exempt a homestead of 200 acres and town and city lots up to $2000 in value.[51] It is true that in 1843 the Supreme Court of the United States held that a stay-law of Illinois was unconstitutional as applied to prior contracts, on the ground that it was an impairment of obligation of contract; and in 1844, it made the same decision as to another Illinois stay-and-appraisal-law; and in 1845, it held invalid a similar Indiana law.[52] These decisions, however, were rendered in suits in the inferior Federal Courts, and held that the invalid State process laws were not binding on parties in such Courts; but these decisions did not necessarily control the State Courts, and in a notable decision in Pennsylvania, Chief Justice Gibson refused to hold a temporary stay-law of that State unconstitutional, saying:[53]

To hold that a State Legislature is incompetent to relieve the public from the pressure of sudden distress by arresting a general sacrifice of property, by the machinery of the law, would invalidate many statutes whose constitutionality has hitherto been unsuspected.

And Chief Justice Dixon in a later case in Wisconsin held similar views as to a law extending the time in foreclosure proceedings, saying: [54]

Although such changes are in general exceedingly unwise and unjust, yet if from sudden and unlooked-for reverses or misfortune, or any other cause, the existing remedies become so stringent in all or a particular class of actions that great and extensive sacrifices of property will ensue, without benefit to the creditor or relief to the debtor, a relaxation of the remedies becomes a positive duty which the State owes to its citizens. . . . In passing upon questions like the present, Courts must look behind the statute itself and take notice of the causes which led to its enactment; for otherwise, they would be unable to determine whether its regulations are reasonable or not, or were demanded by the state of the times or the financial situation of the country. . . . I cannot say that the delay occasioned by it is so great or so unreasonable that it so obstructs or embarrasses proceedings for foreclosure on the part of the mortgagee as to make it under any circumstances unconstitutional and void.

Alabama, Mississippi, and Minnesota also did not accept the doctrine of the United States Supreme Court.[55] The Courts of other States, however, held their State stay-laws invalid.

But here again, it should be noted, there appears a phase of the operation of law which will not be found noticed in the law books, yet which has had much to do with the practical effect of Constitutional doctrines. It is this. These adverse Federal and State decisions did not, in fact, cause great hardship to debtors, because, by reason of the intervals of time which elapsed between enactment of these stay-laws and the Courts' decisions as to their invalidity, the laws to a great extent achieved their main purpose of preventing sacrifice of debtor's property. That phase of the situation may have some bearing on the conditions at the present day. For we have here a perfect example of the fact that law in books and law in operation are often two different things; and especially is this true of Constitutional law. To illustrate these temporarily beneficial delays in judicial processes, it may be noted that the Illinois stay-and-appraisal-laws were in operation two and three years, and the Indiana law four years, before they were held invalid by the United States Supreme Court; the Indiana stay-law of 1842 was not held invalid by the State Court until 1846; an Iowa stay-and-appraisal-law of 1843 was not held invalid by its State Court until 1854; a Michigan mortgage-redemption law of 1843 was not held invalid until 1848, and its stay-and-appraisal-law of 1841 not until 1845; a California mortgage-redemption law of 1851, not until 1854; a Minnesota mortgage-redemption law of 1858 not until 1860; an Alabama two-year redemption law of 1842 was upheld in the State Court in 1858 and not held invalid in the United States Supreme Court until 1860.[56]

One other condition rendered the need for a National bankruptcy law less obvious to many throughout the country, viz., the growth in the number of State insolvency laws. Prior to 1840, less than one half of the States possessed such a law; but after 1840 many more passed this kind of legislation; Pennsylvania adopted an insolvency law in 1836 and again in 1842; Georgia in 1851; Missouri and California in 1852; Connecticut in 1853; Maryland and North Carolina in 1854; Kentucky in 1855.[57] There was, of course, a very great variety in these statutes — some only discharged the person from debt; some, both person and property; some provided for only voluntary bankruptcy; others for both voluntary and involuntary; some provided for hardly more than assignments for benefit of creditors; some required the consent of creditors, and others did not. Moreover, all these State insolvent laws were partial in their operation; for under the decisions of the United States Supreme Court, no such State law could discharge a debtor from debts due to citizens of other States. Yet in spite of these defects and the varying conditions in the different States, the people in general for fifteen years rested content with their imperfect and, in most cases, unjust State laws as to creditor and debtor. Then came the Panic of 1857; and at once there arose a new demand for National protection to creditors and National relief to debtors. The situation which gave rise to such demand was described by an editorial in *Harper's Weekly*, October 10, 1857, in terms which seem like an anticipation of the situation seventy-five years later:

It is a gloomy moment in history. Not for many years, not in the lifetime of most men who read this paper, has there been so much grave and deep apprehension; never has the future seemed so incalculable as at this time. In our own country, there is universal commercial prostration and panic, and thousands of our poorest fellow-citizens are turned out against the approaching Winter without employment, and without the prospect of it. In France, the political caldron seethes and bubbles with uncertainty; Russia hangs, as usual, like a cloud, dark and silent upon the horizon of Europe, while all the energies, resources, and influences of the British Empire are sorely tried, and are yet to be tried more sorely, in coping with the vast and deadly Indian insurrection and with its disturbed relations in China. . . . Of our own troubles, no man can see the end. . . . The very haste to be rich, which is the occasion of this widespread calamity, has also tended to destroy the moral forces with which we are to resist and subdue the calamity. . . .

Under such conditions, men again turned to Congress for relief.

III

THE PERIOD OF NATIONAL INTEREST
1861–1935

THE CIVIL WAR AND THE ACT OF 1867

THE PANIC OF 1873 AND REPEAL

THE SOUTH AND WEST FOR THE DEBTOR

THE DEPRESSION OF 1893–1897 AND THE ACT OF 1898

EXPANSION OF THE BANKRUPTCY POWER

III

THE PERIOD OF NATIONAL INTEREST
1861–1935

THE Panic of 1857, like the previous panics in our history, brought about renewed public discussion of the need of a bankruptcy law.[1] President Buchanan in his First Annual Message, December 8, 1857, attributed most of the country's troubles to the banks, saying:

> It is easy to account for our financial history for the last forty years. It has been a history of extravagant expansions in the business of the country, followed by ruinous contractions. At successive intervals the best and most enterprising men have been tempted to their ruin by excessive bank loans of mere paper credit, exciting them to extravagant importations of foreign goods, wild speculations, and ruinous and demoralizing stock gambling. When the crisis arrives, as arrive it must, the banks can extend no relief to the people. In a vain struggle to redeem their liabilities in specie they are compelled to contract their loans and their issues, and at last, in the hour of distress, when their assistance is most needed, they and their debtors together sink into insolvency.

And though Buchanan, in 1827 and in 1841, had been foremost in opposing any kind of National bankruptcy law whatever, he now recommended a limited law applicable only to banks:

Congress, in my opinion, possess the power to pass a uniform bankrupt law applicable to all banking institutions throughout the United States, and I strongly recommend its exercise. This would make it the irreversible organic law of each bank's existence that a suspension of specie payments shall produce its civil death. The instinct of self-preservation would then compel it to perform its duties in such a manner as to escape the penalty and preserve its life.

In May, 1858, however, James A. Bayard of Delaware in the Senate reported from the Judiciary Committee that "they are unable to agree upon the terms of a bankrupt law, differing principally upon a cardinal question, a majority being opposed to any law embodying a system of voluntary bankruptcy." Hannibal Hamlin of Maine wanted extra copies of the minority report printed, saying that "we have calls for it all over the country"; but Trusten Polk of Missouri said a great majority of the people in the Western States "felt no interest in the matter." In the House, a report was made adverse to the President's proposal.[2] And so nothing was done by Congress to relieve the distress. For three years, Congress callously omitted to take any action,[3] though the number of failures continued very large, particularly in the States of the middle West. It is interesting to note that from 1857 to 1861, the failures in the Middle States ($377,000,000) were nearly three times those of the Eastern States ($140,500,000); the Western States came next ($154,000,000); and the Southern States had the fewest failures ($87,000,000). Then, in 1861, just when business was beginning to

revive from the effects of the Panic of 1857, the out-
break of the Civil War gave rise to great commercial
distress. The planters and traders of the South were
largely indebted to Northern merchants, and their
debts were suddenly and completely wiped out.[4] This
indebtedness of the South to the North in 1861
was carefully estimated at $300,000,000, of which
$159,000,000 was due to New York, $24,100,000
to Philadelphia, $19,000,000 to Baltimore, and
$7,600,000 to Boston; and the practical annihilation
of this large amount of assets produced widespread,
undeserved, and unexpected insolvency in the chief
commercial cities of the North. In 1861, 913 mercantile houses in New York became insolvent with
liabilities in no case under $50,000. Out of 256 sol-
vent dry goods houses in New York at the beginning
of the war, only 16 were solvent at the end of the
first year.[5]

Dun's Commercial Agency reported failures as

Year	Number	Amount
1857	4,932	$290,750,000
1858	4,225	94,749,662
1859	3,913	64,394,000
1860	3,676	79,807,845
1861	6,993	207,210,427

Of the 6,993 insolvencies in 1861, 5,935 were in the
Northern States and 1,088 in the Southern.

Under these circumstances, Congress should have
moved; but its non-action was thus explained by
Roscoe Conkling of New York:

The commercial disasters of 1857 had occasioned a
demand for a bankruptcy law more or less extensive

97

throughout the country. At the extra session of July, 1861, many petitions numerously signed were introduced. The unexpected brevity of that session and its throng of urgent duties afforded ample apology to petitioners and others for denying the subject final consideration then. The Judiciary Committee was fully occupied with grave and immediate questions and it was thought wise to intrust this subject to a Select Committee of five. After the adjournment, the Committee gathered with some labor from at home and from abroad the materials that would aid them to decide wisely whether the report should be favorable or not.

Congress did not even find the time to consider bills introduced in both Senate and House in the spring of 1862 "for the relief of honest but unfortunate debtors." [6] In December, 1862, and January, 1863, however, bills introduced by Lafayette S. Foster of Connecticut in the Senate and by Conkling in the House were vigorously debated. Foster stated that:

For two years past, trade and business have been so embarrassed in this country that failures among mercantile men, indeed among all men who were engaged in any trade or business, have been greatly more numerous than they ever were before in this country, great as have been the previous shocks to business and credit. The failures in 1861, where the liabilities were over $5,000 each, amount, from returns actually made, to nearly 9,000 representing an amount of debts between $200,000,000 and $300,000,000. . . . The number of bankrupts under these circumstances is thousands. . . . The great mass are, I believe honestly, hopelessly insolvent. It is desirable that we should relieve them of an intolerable burden.

98

Considerable objection to the bill developed in the Senate. John P. Hale of New Hampshire stated his fears that if it should be passed, so near to the close of this Congress, it would "enter into the political discussions of the ensuing summer and if it be not repealed by the next Congress, it will be an element in the canvass that is to decide the next Presidency. I fear it will be made a party question, and, however upright and pure may have been the conduct and motives of those who pass it, it will be assailed, it will be denounced as an aristocratic measure, a measure for the benefit of speculators and ruined merchants; and the vulgar prejudices of the populace will be appealed to, and an excitement will be created, the result of which would be that it would be repealed and that would be the end of a bankrupt law for another half century at least. . . . A bankrupt bill should be considered on its purely mercantile and beneficent operations, not brought into the arena of party politics. I exceedingly fear that the passage of a bankrupt bill by this Congress at this time will be disastrous to the hopes of those who desire it incorporated permanently into the legislation of the country."

One hitherto much disputed question cropped up, namely, how far the bill should extend to corporations. The failure to include them had been a strong argument against the Act of 1841. The present bill included only business corporations. Lyman Trumbull of Illinois moved to extend it to banking and railroad corporations — a motion which was defeated by a vote of 17 to 18. Jacob Collamer of Vermont and Trumbull moved to exclude municipal corporations, which was agreed to.

Another subject of hot dispute was a proposal which greatly perturbed this and all succeeding bankruptcy debates. After the Act of 1841, many States had exempted from execution varying amounts of homestead and other real and personal property of debtors; and the existence of such exemptions constituted one reason why debtors were reconciled to the absence of any National bankruptcy law prior to the Civil War. (The subject of property exemption in its historical aspect has never been properly described and should be the subject of thorough research.[7]) James R. Doolittle of Wisconsin now moved that all debtors' property so exempted by the States should be free from the demands of creditors under the National bankruptcy law. To this, objection was strongly made that, as these exemptions were very different in the several States, their allowance would render the law non-uniform and that Congress had no power so to discriminate in favor of more property in one State than in another, and thus to benefit debtors in one State more than in another. This proposal for exemptions was defeated by a vote of 11 to 26; and this led to the postponement of all action on the bill by the Senate, the Western States being unwilling to accept any bankruptcy bill which did not include a provision for such exemptions. In the House, Conkling's bill (which, be it noted, excluded the rebels of the South from its benefits) was laid on the table after long debate, although Conkling earnestly contended that "now more than ever, it is to the public interest that all the energies of the country should be free," and that a mass of men loaded with debt would impede the progress of the war. And further, he urged that it was of great importance to strike down "that system of accommodation and indorsements which as a means of creating credit is so hurtful a source of fictitious capital, enabling men without substance or stability of their own, to establish a baseless and unreal position and to draw in the community by appearances utterly deceptive," and he urged further that a uniform bankruptcy system would "strike at all preferential assignments, etc., made to the exclusion and robbery of some creditors." The failure of the bill "was viewed with much regret by a very large portion of the citizens of this country," said a writer in New York. "Such a measure can have but two classes of opponents — the grasping creditor who has the unfortunate debtor within his power to the exclusion of others, and the dishonest debtor who wishes to hasten the day of reckoning with those he has systematically defrauded." [8] It was asserted that there were over 100,000 insolvent debtors in the loyal States.

The next year, 1864, Thomas A. Jenckes of Rhode Island reported in the House a very carefully drawn bill (of 74 pages), based on a liberal theory, with an improved machinery for administration, and establishing a permanent bankruptcy system, free from

101

political or partisan aims. It applied to corporations, and for the first time it provided that with the assent of his creditors a debtor might wind up his affairs under a trust deed, with the same effect as if by the Court. (A similar proposal had been made but defeated in the debate on Hayne's bankruptcy bill in 1827.) Jenckes strongly urged its passage, saying that "Never was there an occasion when the passage of such a law was so necessary nor the demand so urgent. Thousands were wrecked in the Panic of 1857 who have never yet regained a firm foothold in any business. Thousands more were stranded in the repudiation by Southern debtors in 1860." A motion was made by James F. Wilson of Iowa to amend the bill so as to extend provisions to municipal and other corporations, which Jenckes refused, saying: "It will not do, to destroy the local governments of any portion of the country." James A. Garfield of Ohio opposed the bill's consideration at that time; and James A. Cravens of Indiana (Democrat) was opposed to its adoption at any time, saying that "the Western people without respect to party do not desire its passage, particularly the agriculturists, and there have been no petitions from the West." This statement was denied by others. Cravens also assailed the bill, as "adding another incentive to profligacy and to the reckless speculation which now rages like a fever and deranges the public mind to an alarming extent." After a rejection of the bill by the close vote of 64 to 65, the House finally reconsidered; and at the next session, it was finally passed on

December 12, 1864, by a vote of 76 to 56. The Senate, however, failed to act.[9] One of the chief causes of its failure was the opposition of the Boston Board of Trade and other Northern commercial bodies to any such legislation, until the ending of the war and the reconstruction of the Southern States under the Constitution.[10]

In May, 1866, in the next (39th) Congress, the war being over, the Jenckes bill was again reported to the House, its author stating that it had received universal favor from the mercantile interests and the general advocacy of the press. As in the case of previous bills, forty and twenty-five years before, there were four factions in Congress — those who opposed any bankruptcy law at all, those who opposed any bill providing for involuntary bankruptcy, those who favored a bill largely for benefit of creditors, those who advocated a complete and permanent bill for both debtor and creditor. To pass the bill, concessions had to be made to each by the other three factions.[11] To appease the debtors, the advocates of the bill accepted, though with grave misgivings as to its constitutionality, a provision applying all State exemptions of property from execution. Such exemptions, said John A. Kasson of Iowa, were "precious to the judgment, conscience, and heart of the Western man," and without them, the bill could not be supported. The so-called creditor class were favored by the inclusion of a provision that no discharge should be granted without assent of a majority of the creditors if the debtor's assets did not pay fifty per cent, but even here a further concession had to be made to the debtor class by a proviso that this clause should not apply to any bankruptcy proceeding begun within one year, and thus should relieve all existing debtors from the necessity of any assent of creditors. With these concessions to both debtors and creditors, the proponents of the bill finally mustered enough votes to pass it by a vote of 68 to 59 in the House, and later on acceptance by the House of the Conference Committee Report by the close vote of 73 to 71.[12] Those who wanted only voluntary bankruptcy held out against the bill to the bitter end, and there was some justice in their position; for this bill in its involuntary section was not confined to traders (as was the Act of 1841) nor did it exempt farmers and laborers (as did the later Act of 1898). To force farmers and mechanics into compulsory bankruptcy is "a preposterous and revolting thing," said Dalbert E. Paine of Wisconsin. The country did not ask for it and "to force it on them is an intolerable, indefensible wrong." "It is peculiarly offensive," he said, "to the free and easy but honest and true men of the West whom it will squeeze into the strait jacket so befitting the madmen of Wall Street. The farmers and mechanics of the West will rise against it. The State laws can do everything for debtor and creditor except to discharge the debtor from prior debts. No new National collection law is needed." To this, Jenckes rightly answered that the very fact that States could not discharge a prior debt or debts due to non-resident creditors made it absolutely necessary, in the interest of both classes, that there should be a uniform law for an equitable distribution of assets and discharge. The House bill was laid on the table by the Senate at this session; but at the next session, in February, 1867, the bill was finally taken up and after a thorough debate, it was passed by the close vote of 22 to 20, becoming the Bankrupt Act of March 2, 1867, c. 176 (15 Stat. 227) — twenty-five years after the repeal of the Act of 1841.[13] Several factors concurred in bringing about this result. The most important among them was the feeling that it would relieve the plight of debtors due to the depreciated condition of the currency. James R. Doolittle of Wisconsin said:

> The circumstances in which the country is now placed, owing to the terrible convulsion through which we have passed, are such and the change of the currency from year to year has been so great, so violent, that the word "dollar" in which all contracts are made and in which they must be enforced has been continually changing in meaning . . . and therefore it is utterly unjust to endeavor to enforce literally contracts which have been made in these times of convulsion. . . . This law will do very much toward bringing peace to the country.

And William M. Stewart of Nevada said the same:

> Throughout the North, values have changed so rapidly in the last six years, men's property has fluctuated to such an extent that there is a large number of persons who are insolvent, with large indebtedness hanging over them, which is merely the result of the fluctuation in prices and which no human foresight could have guarded against. It is highly important that they should be relieved. . . . If

there ever has been a time when a bankrupt bill was appropriate, now is the time. Furthermore, we should have on our statute books a regular system for all time.

The chief pressure for the bill came from Northern creditors of Southern debtors, who saw in it their only chance of getting any pay from these debtors, as the latter owned only landed property, and having control of the Southern Legislatures and Courts were procuring stay-and-exemption-laws unconstitutionally applicable to prior debts.[14] Samuel C. Pomeroy of Kansas said:

There has never been a time for many years past when a man from the North could enforce the collection of a debt there, unless he was of that standing and character which enabled him to have friends and supporters there. I have been associated with men who could not appear in the Courts there, men who believed as I do. There has been no time in 20 years past, or at least within the last 10 years when they could collect a debt there at all.

A vigorous debate arose again in the Senate over an attempt to remove from the bill the section preserving State exemptions of property, on the ground of its unconstitutionality, but William P. Fessenden of Maine set forth the opposite view — a view which the Supreme Court later adopted:

The idea of some gentlemen is that the law, to be uniform, must be equal in its operations. I do not hold to that idea at all. If we make a rule which operates upon the States equally, that is to say, which is equal in its terms, so far as the States are concerned, it would not be unconstitutional simply because, owing to the particular provisions of the several States, the operation would not be precisely similar. The provision of the Constitution unquestionably was intended to apply to the several States to prevent any distinction being made between them.

A motion was made by Reverdy Johnson of Maryland to include in the bill all corporations; and he reviewed the gigantic frauds by corporations "which have done more than anything else to unsettle confidence in the integrity of our people both at home and abroad." He cited the case of the Ohio Trust Company, "receiving millions on deposits, with offices in nearly all the commercial towns of the country and in New York, all of which, by fraudulent misconduct or mistake, became bankrupt and ruined thousands," and, he asked, "how many of the railroad companies and banks have ruined their creditors?" In its final form, the provisions of the bill applied to "moneyed, business, or commercial corporations."

Moved by pressure from the debtors, the Senate struck out the House provision requiring assent of creditors to a discharge, but the Conference Committee restored the provision, without which the House would not pass the bill.

It is significant of the persistence of the bitter war-feelings that, though there had been eliminated from the bill a provision (contained in previous bills) that Southern rebels should not have the benefit of it, efforts were made by Thaddeus Stevens in the House and by Charles Sumner in the Senate either to restore this provision, or to require a test oath of all petitioners in bankruptcy. It had been largely owing to opposition of Republicans holding such views and fearing that a bankruptcy law would chiefly benefit the South that the previous bills had failed.[15] The advocates of the present bill now resented the introduction of this question again, two years after the close of the war; and Jenckes, in the House, replying to the charge by Thaddeus Stevens that the bill might "let some rebels go," asked: "Will Stevens, who so many years has been known as the champion of the black man, now in his old age, vote for the continued enslavement of the white man?" And Luke Poland of Vermont in the Senate, replying to Charles Sumner, said: "The subject of the rebellion and the rebels is connected with almost everything that we have here in the Senate, but I thought that we had at last got upon a bill that would steer entirely clear of it. . . . It seems to me this is carrying the thing altogether too far." "The rebel spirit must be broken down" by all forms of legislation, replied Sumner; and he said: "Horrors exist now, just as in old Kansas days when the slave masters of that time smiled over what they called the 'freedom shriekers of Kansas,' smiled over all the evidence that we introduced day by day of the terrible atrocities that were there perpetrated; and Senators now in similar mood smile when all these horrors are brought before them." James Dixon of Connecticut protested, saying: "The accusation against the whole South is a stupendous falsehood, that they are engaged in one grand conspiracy of oppression and abuse against those who were formerly Union men and against the blacks." The episode was closed by the remark of John Conness of California that "I am tired of the whip of the leader in this body lashed at me, telling the country at the same time in those stentor tones of his that there is none here to do his duty but the honorable gentleman from Massachusetts."

This Bankruptcy Act of 1867, while it became rapidly unpopular, is significant in being the first bill constructed as a permanent piece of legislation and with a view to the interest of the Nation and of National commerce and not merely to the interest of individual debtors and creditors. It is also significant in illustrating the degree to which men's minds had moved forward, in their views of the scope of the Bankruptcy Clause of the Constitution; for all the old questions as to the constitutionality of voluntary bankruptcy, of extension of bankruptcy to any class of persons other than traders, and of its application to corporations — questions which, in the 1820's, 1830's, and 1840's, had caused such heated contests — now aroused practically no debate.[16] The country had expanded and the Constitution had kept pace with it. (It is interesting to note that the questions as to constitutionality were not finally set at rest by the Supreme Court until 1902 in the case of *Hanover National Bank* v. *Moyses*.)

The Act of 1867 had hardly been enacted, however, before pressure began to be brought to mitigate its features in the further interest of the debtors. In 1868 an act was passed, over the strong protest of representatives of the creditors, to extend until Januuary 1, 1869, the exemption of bankrupts from the requirement as to assent of creditors to a discharge.[17] In 1872 an act was passed to grant to them further favor, by a provision that in all bankruptcy cases the State exemptions of property in force in 1871 should apply.[18] The original Act of 1867 applied to State exemptions existing in 1864; but in 1864 many of the States were regarded as out of the Union, and their Constitutions and laws illegal and of no effect. Since the war, all the Southern and many Western States had adopted new constitutions and statutes providing for exemptions of property from execution; and as these exemptions had been greatly increased in amounts, the debtors saw great advantage in having the Bankruptcy Act amended. To understand how greatly they benefited, it should be noted that Arkansas exempted a homestead of $5,000 and personalty of $2,000; Georgia, a homestead of $2,000 and personalty of $1,000; Florida, a homestead of $16,000 and personalty of $1,000; Louisiana, a homestead of $16,000 and personalty of $2,000; Mississippi, a homestead of 240 acres and personalty of $4,000; in North Carolina and South Carolina, a homestead of $1,000 and personalty of $500; in Virginia, a homestead and personalty of $2,000; in Kansas, a homestead of $5,000 and personalty of over $1,200; in Texas, a homestead of 200 acres and town and city lots up to $2,000 in value.[19]

In connection with this Act of 1872, a curious and unique episode in legislative history ensued. After the State exemptions of 1871 were thus incorporated in the Bankrupt Law, various State Courts (notably Virginia) held that their State exemption laws did not apply to debts incurred prior to their passage, and that if they were to be so construed as to apply they would be unconstitutional. This was undoubtedly good law; but if enforced in cases under the National Bankruptcy Act, it would defeat the object of Congress in granting to debtors such exemptions. Accordingly, a peculiar statute was passed on March 3, 1873, not only declaring "the true intent and meaning" of the Act of 1872 but also further enacting that the State exemptions existing in 1871 should be valid against prior debts, "any decision of any such (State) Court rendered since the adoption and passage of such (State) Constitution and laws to the contrary notwithstanding." [20] In the Senate, Bayard of Delaware strongly challenged the constitutional power of Congress to pass such a bill, saying:

It is sought by means of a Congressional Act to do that which would be in violation of the policy which placed the restriction upon the States. However much I may desire to see ease and favor granted to debtors at the present time and under the emergencies of the losses entailed by the entire disruption of their system of labor and their social economies throughout the Southern States, I cannot but look with disfavor upon this method of running to Congress to obtain a reversal of the deliberate and in my opinion just decisions of their State Courts. I confess that, with all my sympathy for this class of struggling debtors, I feel that this bill is in violation of a constitutional limitation. . . . Believing that the obligation of a contract is essential to be preserved, and as men must be held to make their contracts in view of the law as it exists, for the

111

public law enters of its own force into every contract, and as these contracts were made in the face of existing law, I shall be sorry to see this measure adopted.

Within a month from the passage of this statute, the Supreme Court in holding invalid a provision of the Georgia Constitution of 1868 increasing exemptions as applied to prior contracts intimated that Congress itself could not "give the slightest effect to a State law or Constitution in conflict with the Constitution of the United States." In 1874, some Circuit Courts of the United States held this Act of 1873 unconstitutional as violating the Due Process Clause; others held it invalid as not being uniform in its exemptions. The Supreme Court never passed upon the question, though in 1878 that Court held all the Southern State exemption laws unconstitutional as applied to prior debts.[21]

In spite of these amendments, the Act of 1867 almost from the outset proved a failure and unpopular everywhere. As time went on, its defects became increasingly evident; and the Supreme Court had occasion to construe it in about 35 cases. Its administration became more and more wasteful. While the number of bankruptcies was not as great as expected, the ratio of voluntary to involuntary was greater (in five years, about 53,000 to 3,300). As reported by the *American Law Review*, from June 1, 1867, to August 31, 1871, the total number of bankruptcies was 103,005, of which 15,151 were in the Eastern States; 24,534 in the Middle States; 22,780 in the Southern States; 40,097 in the Western States; and

433 in the District of Columbia.[22] The fees to the registers and assignees as officers of the Court more and more absorbed the assets; and the average dividends paid to creditors did not exceed ten per cent. As the *American Law Review* said in July, 1873: "From the beginning to the end, there is one continuous, increasing plucking at the estate. Merchants have come to believe it best to settle with their debtors out of the Bankrupt Court. . . . In its details the law is perplexing, cumbersome, annoying, and expensive." [23] The *Review* argued that at least the Registers in Bankruptcy should be appointed by the Judges and for not over three-year terms. "We should not then have (for Registers) broken-down politicians in whom the prickings of the stomach far exceed the prickings of conscience, nor poor, witless nurselings." This, it said, "would sweep away at one blow the greater part of the real and disinterested dissatisfaction with the law as it stands." [24] Extensive fraud, corruption, and misapplication of funds were prevalent in the Federal Courts held by carpet-bag Judges in Louisiana and other Southern States; and it was said that in New Orleans out of 1,800 bankruptcies, in only one was any substantial dividend realized.[25] These conditions disgusted and inflamed Northern creditors against the Act itself. Another reason for the Act's unpopularity with debtors was a construction which the Supreme Court in 1871 (in *Toof* v. *Martin*, 13 Wall. 40) put upon the word "insolvency." To the ordinary man that word denoted lack of assets of value sufficient to pay debts;

113

but the Court held it to mean inability to pay debts as they become due in ordinary course of business. This definition, while possibly suited to commercial men in the cities, was utterly out of line with the usual business methods of the farmers, planters, and country merchants. And still another leading reason for the Act's unpopularity was the general prevalence in the West and South of the view that the whole course of legislation since the war had gone too far in increasing the powers and jurisdiction of the Federal Courts and in removing cases out of the State Courts. Dissatisfaction reached such a pitch that the House of Representatives, in January, 1873, passed a bill for the repeal of the Act, without debate and by a two-thirds vote.[26] Nine months later, the Panic of 1873 broke over the land, precipitated by the failure of Jay Cooke and Company on September 18. "To the reckless mismanagement of that firm, its hazarding the money of its depositors upon imaginary securities, is to be directly attributed the present financial condition of the country — wrecked fortunes, closed manufactories, thousands upon thousands of laboring men thrown out of employment in the winter season of the year, the prices of the produce which is the result of a whole year's labor of the agriculturists diminished until it aggregates millions of loss." So said Ephraim K. Wilson of Maryland, and it was charged by other Congressmen that that failure had been precipitated by a petition in bankruptcy by disgruntled creditors; and that if the Bankruptcy Law had not been in existence, the failure might not

114

have happened.[27] President Grant evidently shared this view, and in his Message of December 1, 1873, he said that he had become impressed with the belief that the Act of 1867 "is productive of more evil than good at this time" and he stated:

Many considerations might be urged for its total repeal, but, if this is not considered advisable, I think it will not be seriously questioned that those portions of said act providing for what is called involuntary bankruptcy operate to increase the financial embarrassments of the country. Careful and prudent men very often become involved in debt in the transaction of their business and though they may possess ample property, if it could be made available for that purpose, to meet all their liabilities, yet, on account of the extraordinary scarcity of money, they may be unable to meet all their pecuniary obligations as they become due, in consequence of which they are liable to be prostrated in their business by proceeding in bankruptcy at the instance of unrelenting creditors. People are now so easily alarmed as to monetary matters that the mere filing of a petition in bankruptcy by an unfriendly creditor will necessarily embarrass, and oftentimes accomplish the financial ruin, of a responsible business man. Those who otherwise might make lawful and just arrangements to relieve themselves from difficulties produced by the present stringency in money are prevented by their constant exposure to attack and disappointment by proceedings against them in bankruptcy, and besides, the law is made use of in many cases by obstinate creditors to frighten or force debtors into a compliance with their wishes and into acts of injustice to other creditors and to themselves. I recommend that so much of said act as provides for involuntary bankruptcy on account of suspension of payments be repealed.

Accordingly, on December 16, 1873, a bill for total repeal was introduced in the House and was passed after only two hours' debate, by a vote of 219 to 44.[28] "In my judgment," said Lyman Tremain of New York, "no measure of relief that this Congress can pass will be hailed with such satisfaction." Hugh I. Jewett of Ohio said:

I believe as a business man that the existence of this bankrupt act is doing more today to continue the present conditions of things in the country than all the stringency in the money market. It is the uncertainty, the doubt, the fear that at an unexpected moment some unyielding creditor will place in bankruptcy the struggling debtor, that the means he has will be taken beyond his control and be absorbed by the proceedings of the Court.

Charles A. Eldredge of Wisconsin said that the law had never been favored by the farmers and that:

It was a scheme devised in the interest of speculators; and its effect has been to encourage speculation and recklessness in the transaction of business. . . . This infernal law would be more properly denominated a confiscation law than a law for the distribution of the assets of the debtor among his creditors.

Clarkson N. Potter of New York favored the retention of voluntary bankruptcy, but said that all the great creditor centers of the country favored repeal of the involuntary feature — New York, Chicago, Philadelphia, and St. Louis. Heretofore, he said, "the frequent practice of the country was for creditors to arrange with their failing debtors according as they found for their common interest. Now, it is placed in the power of one creditor to put the debtor into bankruptcy." Lyman Tremain of New York said:

Under the law as it now stands, any trader or merchant is liable to have his estate thrown into bankruptcy, his pecuniary credit and reputation ruined, and his property subject to ruinous losses and sacrifices, in cases where he is perfectly solvent in the legal sense of the term, where 95 % of his creditors may be averse to any such forcible measure, where if a reasonable time were allowed, he might make an arrangement to pay all his debts and have a handsome surplus left, and where no act of fraud, either of omission or commission, was alleged to have been committed by him. No bankrupt law on earth has been so severe as this. . . . It is enough that any man's commercial paper shall have been unpaid for 14 days . . . his estate is liable to be thrown into bankruptcy. . . . It is believed that the compulsory operations of this law and the fact of its existence tended very greatly to aggravate the recent panic, commencing in New York and extending to other commercial centers and finally prevailing to a greater or less extent, throughout the length and breadth of the land.

That the conditions of the times clearly demanded relief to debtors may be seen from the leading editorial of *The Nation* in New York, May 28, 1874, which showed that the effects of the Panic of 1873 had not yet disappeared:

All through the depression of last winter, people flattered themselves that the spring would bring back at least a portion of the usual activity, and that before summer, we should be in a fair way to forget our woes. These expectations have not been realized. The dullness in every branch of industry is very great. Even stock speculation . . . is

117

almost extinct. . . . There is greater depression than in 1858;
the process of recovery has thus far been slower, the commercial activity of the community appears to be smaller.
. . . There is more doubt about the future than there was
after the last panic, and a greater hesitation about entering
on enterprises requiring a long period for the completion.

This repeal bill, passed by the House "with inconsiderate haste," as the *American Law Review* said, received a "thorough and enlightened consideration in
the Senate, especially by Senators Edmund and Thurman." [29] In that body, the repeal clause was struck
out from the House bill, and with several important
amendments to the Act of 1867, the bill became the
Act of June 22, 1874. Chief of the amendments, and
the most debated, was a provision for composition,
based on the English Bankruptcy Act of 1869. This
was an entirely new feature, although something of
the kind had been proposed by Robert Y. Hayne as
an amendment to the 1827 bill. In explanation of it,
George F. Edmunds of Vermont said:

. . . As this is dealing with private rights, and not in
view of immediate liquidation as in bankruptcy, it may go
on for ten years, if you please, if the requisite number
agree to it, and is therefore compelling a minority who do
not, it may be, agree to it at all. It is still necessary that it
shall be presented to the judge and that he shall be satisfied
that all these steps have been complied with in the first
place, and in the second place that it is a fair and honest
composition to make. . . . The Court must be satisfied, in
short, that every man who stands out against such a proposition as this and against the will of the great bulk of the
creditors and the debtor, must stand out for some selfish
and captious reason. In other words, to reverse the state-

ment, the Court must be satisfied that the composition proper is a just and honest one, and is for the real benefit of the whole body of creditors alike, and of the debtor, and of course that the composition shall be equal, that nobody shall get an advantage over another.

Many doubts were expressed in the Congress, in the press, and among lawyers as to the constitutionality of this provision, since it was not such a bankruptcy law as was known at the time of the framing of the Constitution. To such attacks, Allen G. Thurman of Indiana made an eloquent and convincing reply:

. . . It is not sufficient that such a law as we now have before us may not have been particularly within the mind of the framers of the Constitution, or even of the American people, when they adopted that instrument; if the bill is within the language of the Constitution, and is consistent with the other provisions of the Constitution, is not repugnant to the letter or spirit of the Constitution, and is warranted expressly by its language, then the bill is constitutional, although that particular measure was not in the minds of the framers of the Constitution or of the American people, when that instrument was framed. It was upon that argument precisely that the voluntary clause in the bankrupt law was sustained by those who advocated it, that it was the intention of the framers of the Constitution, for the reasons which induced them to put that clause in the Constitution at all, to give Congress power to make uniform laws on the subject of men who failed in business, who were bankrupts, who were bankrupts in the most popular sense of the term, as well as in the technical sense of the term, men who attempted fraudulently to deprive creditors of their rights, or who were unable to meet their obligations in the due and ordinary course of business, and that the whole subject being thus

119

confided to the jurisdiction of Congress, it was no answer to say that this particular measure for such a class of cases, cases of bankruptcy, cases of individuals unable to meet their obligations in the ordinary course of business, was not in the contemplation of those who framed the Constitution of the United States.

It was not until 1881 that the Supreme Court recognized the constitutionality of this composition provision, and similar recognition has been given in many later cases.[30]

The Act of 1874 contained many other amendments of the original law, and all of them passed to mitigate the situation of debtors. One of these provided that no one should be adjudged a bankrupt compulsorily except on petition of one quarter in number and one half in amount of creditors. Another amendment which became peculiarly obnoxious to creditors was as follows. The bill, as it passed the House, had abolished, as to pending cases of involuntary bankruptcy only, the requirement of the original Act of 1867 (as amended in 1868) for an assent of a majority in number and value of creditors to the discharge of either a voluntary or an involuntary bankrupt if his assets did not equal thirty per cent of his liabilities. This abolition had been hotly attacked by some members of the House, who charged that the bill so providing had been framed by attorneys of Jay Cooke & Co., to facilitate the discharge of that firm, and that it was "manifestly the emanation of that firm and their fraudulent brethren, intended to whitewash the gigantic frauds perpetrated by the bankruptcy and rail-

road corporations which have brought us to the verge
of bankruptcy." [31] The Senate adopted this provision, but applied it to all future cases as well as to
pending cases; on the other hand, it required for the
discharge of voluntary bankrupts, assent of one
quarter in number and one third in amount. "This
is a premium on staying out of bankruptcy which will
not benefit either debtors or creditors," said the
American Law Review. "Besides, as soon as this law
is thoroughly understood every bankrupt will take
care that some friendly creditor files a bill against
him, and the law requiring assent of creditors will be
practically repealed." The bill as finally passed, the
American Law Review said, "does much to destroy
the efficiency of the law and little or nothing to
remedy the evils of which the country complained.
. . . It is certainly intended to suppress voluntary
bankrupts. The whole result of these provisions must
be to encourage fraud and preference and to delay
honest men in attempting to collect their debts.
That provision which enables a majority of creditors
to compel the assent of a minority to a composition
is of doubtful constitutionality." Judge John Lowell
wrote that the discharge provisions were "an extraordinary law — a compliance with the pressure of
the times — which operates with a perverse ingenuity
to discourage honest debtors coming into the bankrupt Court and to throw insuperable obstacles in the
way of bringing a fraudulent debtor there." [32]

   In spite of the concessions to the debtors in the
Act of 1874, and, in part, because of them, the de-

mand for repeal of the whole bankruptcy legislation became overwhelming from all over the country, and it was endorsed by the Legislatures of New York, Kentucky, New Hampshire, Illinois, Indiana, Mississippi, and other States. Accordingly, in April, 1878, a repeal bill introduced by James R. McCreary of Kentucky was adopted by the Senate after only two days' debate, and by the House with but one day's debate, by a vote of 205 to 40.[33] "The day has passed for the bankruptcy law," said William P. Whyte of Maryland in the Senate. "It has accomplished its mission. The war had brought hundreds of thousands to the verge of bankruptcy and relief was needed as a sponge for past indebtedness. The Act has done its work." The Act now, said McCreary, is merely an "assault upon public morals, in its violations of good faith, in its craft, its falsehoods and frauds." And the arguments against any bankruptcy legislation were expressed by John A. McMahon of Ohio, who said:

I believe a bankrupt law as a permanent institution in this country is to a certain extent contrary to the spirit of our institutions. It is not adapted to a country like this where the great mass of our people are farmers, and where even a large portion of the persons engaged in commercial pursuits have never been educated up to the high idea of commercial promptness that exists in the cities of New York and Boston and notably in the cities of Great Britain. A bankrupt law has, therefore, always been against the sentiment of the people of the West and against the sentiment of a great portion of the people of the South as a permanent institution. In the second place, it has been a

122

failure in practice. The average per cent of distribution of assets has not exceeded 10–15 %. Its cost is also great. An insolvent debtor lives out of his estate up to the last moment until finally, there is nothing left but the shell. I favor, however, postponement of operation of repeal. We are entering upon a period of increased business depression, when we are constantly witnessing further decline in value. Postpone for a year so that this country may realize, before the voluntary feature is repealed, the full extent of the depression in business and decline in values. I think that this much is due to the commercial and manufacturing classes, because it is by the legislation of Congress that this condition of affairs has been in part brought about.

The interesting fact clearly appeared in the debates, as John J. Ingalls of Kansas said, that the clamor for repeal came chiefly from creditors and not from debtors. There were some Congressmen, however, who thought that repeal would injure the debtors. "We have not yet got from under the great business depression caused by the revulsion of 1873," said David Davis of Illinois. "Thousands of men are still struggling to pay their debts." And George F. Hoar of Massachusetts thought that "now is a very inopportune time for repeal when our business future is so doubtful and hazardous." The fact was that the depression following the Panic of 1873 was still in full force, after five years' continuance. James Ford Rhodes has described the condition of affairs at this time as follows: "After the presidential election and the almost contemporary closing of the World's Fair in 1876, there was no mitigation of the terrible distress. Masses of laborers were out of employment being severely put to it to get bread for their wives, children and selves. Merchants and manufacturers had difficulty in making both ends meet; many failed; one failure led to another and financial and commercial solvency seemed to be a dream of the past. There was no relief in sight. The European countries were alike suffering and had not the power, if they had the desire, to purchase American securities and thus give a lift to affairs in the United States. The days from November 1876 to the spring of 1879 were dreary and apparently there was not a ray of light. Failures and suspensions of payment of manufacturers and traders, receiverships of railroads were the rule. Croakers predicted universal bankruptcy and it was difficult to traverse such a prediction. . . . Soon after the settlement of the disputed presidency came the railroad strike and riots of 1877." [34] Moreover, the legislation providing for resumption of specie payments was causing a contraction severely felt by the debtor classes. "Just when debtors are complaining of hardship due to contractions of currency and raise in the value of gold, it is contemplated taking away their right to relief from debt," protested Senator Stanley Matthews of Ohio, in opposing repeal of the bankruptcy law. "I know of no period in the history of our country in which it seems to me to be less opportune to take away all of that remedial system which belongs to a scheme of bankruptcy. There never was a time when there was more debt, a larger number of debtors, more insolvency apprehended than exists today." In the House,

Benjamin F. Butler of Massachusetts said that "whatever the cause, inflation or otherwise, men's debts have increased and they are unable to pay." He deplored the shortness of the debate, contended that the cry for repeal was an artificial one, propagated largely by the newspapers, and he said:

This House is governed by newspapers, and not by reason and debate. Members are frightened at their shadow. . . . We spend a day over a dog fight, but not one hour over a great measure of legislation. We gather ourselves about speakers advocating something in regard to a little troutbrook, and leave a whole river of corruption to continue flowing, without consideration or debate.

The pro-silver men in the House were the especial antagonists of repeal. "When resumption comes about, there will be a much larger depreciation in values and many men now engaged in prosperous business will be obliged to seek the benefit of this Act," said John A. McMahon of Ohio. "You propose to repeal this law," said William D. Kelley of Pennsylvania, "at a time when the American people have never been in so great a commercial and manufacturing crisis as they now are. They were never suffering under a more portentous one than that which now overwhelms them. . . . When was business ever so stagnant? The public revenues are shrinking all the time. Do not force business men into the ranks of those who look on our Government as an oppressor, and upon Congress as a wrong-doer. I beg you not to give to the discontented people disciplined and intelligent captains to lead them into open revolt. . . .

The cause of the fall of prices was the action of the United States and Germany in thrusting silver out of the category of money metals. They thus decreed the terrible shrinkage of prices and consequent ruin which have taken place in America and Europe." On the other hand, William P. Frye of Maine said that he did not believe that the return to resumption was "the cause of the widespread ruin in this country today. . . . Else why do you find it in Canada, in England? Why do you find today that out of 116 cotton mills in one city in England 100 of them have stopped?" And Abram D. Hewitt of New York, while believing that unless the Act could be properly amended it should be repealed, said that he nevertheless was convinced that "we are marching speedily and surely back to prosperity. . . . Gentlemen seem to think the distress in this country with the attendant shrinkage of values is something local. Let me tell them that this condition of things exists all over the civilized globe. . . . The business depression and shrinkage of values are not local but universal. They are the reaction from a speculative era; and when you have had an era of speculation, there is no remedy, but through much tribulation, through shrinkage, through liquidation of indebtedness, to get back to the point where we can begin upon the foundation of solid and real values and upon honest and true money." Omar D. Conger of Michigan thought despondingly that repeal of voluntary bankruptcy was inadvisable, in view of the efforts "of communists, free traders, inflationists, and representatives of all those political issues which threaten destruction to all the general interests and stability of the country. ... We have arrived only at the beginning of the troubles of our finances and of our labor question in this country," said he. "We must go through the valley of doubt, of uncertainty, of greatly increased lack of confidence in the public mind, beyond what we have already passed through, if that be possible."

The repeal of the Bankruptcy Act of 1867 was greeted with enthusiasm throughout the country; and Senator John Sherman said in a speech to the Cincinnati Chamber of Commerce in August, 1878: "I think it a hopeful fact that, after this week, there will be an end of bankruptcies, that all men who believe they are not in a condition to pay their debts will have taken the benefit of the law provided for their relief, and after Saturday next, we will all stand upon a better basis — on the basis of our property and our deserved credit."

So lasting was the impression made by the waste and frauds and defective machinery of the Bankruptcy Act of 1867 that, as late as 1893, it was stated in Congress that "the prejudices created by the abuses under the Act of 1867 make a fair discussion of any bankrupt act difficult." [35] Its unpopularity was not due to its harshness toward debtors, but its excessive cost to creditors through unbearable fees and delays, coupled with the fact that in the South, it was administered by "a lot of irresponsible carpet-bag Judges who brought the Courts of the United States with contempt with the people." [36] On the other hand, there were some men who thought that the law had been beneficial in their States; and in 1890, Thomas C. Catchings of Mississippi so stated and expressed a belief that the repeal had been made "in pursuance of a sort of prejudice or craze which had no foundation in fact but which seemed to have taken possession of Congress"; and Ezra B. Taylor of Ohio made the same statement.[37] This view, however, has been shared by few.

Within a year after repeal, however, a movement was started by commercial organizations throughout the country for the passage of a new bill. But there was little general public demand for such legislation; for the unexpected had happened to business, and, as Rhodes said in his history: "In the darkest hour, when predictions were made freely that there could be no revival, the revival came, but men in actual business did not perceive it." In 1880, the Senate referred the subject of bankruptcy to a Committee for investigation; and in December, 1882, John J. Ingalls of Kansas reported a simple bill based on what was known as the Equity System, providing for assignments for benefit of creditors under State laws to be filed by a debtor in a Federal Court, and followed by a marshalling of assets by the Court and a discharge in case no fraud was shown.[38]

A sudden change of mind now took place on the part of Southern and Western Senators, as the necessity for some bankruptcy law under then recent economic conditions became evident. As Senator Garland of Arkansas said: "The calamities inflicted upon the country by the general drought in the year preceding sent up a demand for the passage of an Act. . . . I think it is now a settled conviction in the country that, whether under the influence of a long drought, whether under the influence of adversity or prosperity, good crop or short crops, a great country like this with its foreign or interstate commerce needs a fixed, permanent Act of bankruptcy; and now it is best made in times of peace and prosperity and not in a stampede brought about by the reverses of short crops, etc." Senator Hoar of Massachusetts introduced in opposition to the Committee's measure, a bill based on the insolvency law of that State, and drafted by John Lowell, a distinguished United States District Judge of Boston. It is interesting to note that Ingalls classed among the opponents to bankruptcy legislation "the great wholesale merchants in the chief distributing centers"; for, said he, "they have their agents and attorneys in the vicinity of every debtor, obtaining early information of approaching disaster and ready to avail themselves of the local machinery of State Courts by attachments or by preferences, through which they can secure full payment of their claims to the exclusion of less powerful or less vigilant but equally meritorious creditors. Naturally, they want no bankrupt law at all." [39] There were many objections to the Ingalls bill of a legal nature; and the Senate postponed all action.

In the next (48th) Congress, in 1884, Senator Hoar again reported the bill drafted by Judge Lowell, but with many improvements. The voluntary sections applied only to persons owing over $500, and the involuntary were confined to traders (though this term was very broadly defined). A provision which allowed to the Court a discretion to compute the assets of the debtor as compared with his debts, and to permit him to go for 90 days to see if he could meet his obligations, met with favor from those who objected to the definition of insolvency which the Supreme Court had laid down. This provision is to be noted as containing the germ of the moratorium principle contained in the Ingalls bill of 1882 and in recent legislation on the subject. The Senate passed the bill by a vote of 32 to 15, with most of the Southerners still in opposition; but the bill failed to pass the House.[40] Many men thought that it was improper to press it on the eve of a Presidential election. Patrick A. Collins of Massachusetts, in advocating its passage as necessary under existing conditions "in the interest of commercial honesty," pointed to the prevalence of speculation and to the very recent failure of Grant, Ward & Co. (in May, 1884), "the most stupendous speculation and the most gigantic and disgraceful failure in this country's history. . . . Under our present system, no honest debtor can be freed from obligations outside his State, and no rascal can be punished for his swindling." Albert A. Willis of Kentucky, on the other hand, contended that the people did not want a bankruptcy law, that the different State exemptions of property made such a law unfair and non-uniform in its operation, and that the law would only foster the present reign of speculation and dishonesty; and he described vividly the "fiery, rabid, quenchless, lust of gold which has excited a spirit of rash speculation that from time to time has raged like an infection throughout the land. The beet-root frenzy when the cry everywhere was 'make sugar and get rich', the vine excitement during which the culture of corn and cotton among our Southern planters was abandoned in favor of the grape, the silk worm or mulberry mania of the past, the gold and stock gambling of the present day. . . . We see in our midst a spirit of prodigal expenditure and unnecessary extravagance . . . splendid apparel, luxurious seats, retinues of servants and other ostentatious social paraphernalia. . . . 'Live within your means' is ignored or laughed at as an exploded absurdity." Samuel W. Moulton of Illinois opposed any involuntary system of bankruptcy because of changed business conditions. "Formerly, Eastern manufacturers sold direct to merchants and traders of the West," he said, "but of late years, a large jobbing business has sprung up in the West, supplying small traders who are known personally as to financial conditions, habits, etc., to jobbers who can assist them over difficulty of payment. The jobber will be destroyed by this bill; for Eastern manufacturers would have an interest to throw him into bankruptcy, so as to monopolize the entire trade of the country. Easy money in the East makes it easy for Eastern vendors to buy up the paper of the Western jobbers and put them into bankruptcy on failure to pay on the day."

In the next Congress, in 1885–1886, after the election of President Cleveland, Senator Hoar again reported his bill.[41]

"A most vicious bill," Preston B. Plumb of Kansas termed it. "Bad as things are today," he said, "they can be aggravated by the passage of unwise laws, of which this is one. It is a device of Wall St., of the active capital of the country, against its property and its prosperity." Henry M. Teller of Colorado said that there was "never a bill more potent for evil and injustice," and that there was no demand for it in the South or West. "It originated in Boston by men who want to put their grip upon the debtors of the West and South, the men who complain that they cannot get the last pound of flesh and every particle which belongs to them." And he added: "I think now, when all the industries of the country are paralyzed, when the business of the country is in a state that needs assistance, it is no time to pass bills of this character — when every man in trade today (and it has been so for the last three years) is suffering from the depression, from the lack of money, and from the lack of business in this country. . . . A bankrupt law opens the door for a fraudulent debtor and closes it against the honest and deserving debtor." To this, Senator Hoar retorted that he would not term Teller's language "mere railing" but he would call it "mere rhetoric." . . . "The leading merchants and manufacturers of this country are not a set of sharks and Shylocks. They build our railroads, our vast internal commerce. To make an attack of the kind the Senator makes upon them is an attack upon the American character." And Hoar added, with considerable truth:

This legislation is in the interests of the new frontier agricultural communities and the old sparsely settled planting communities of this country, even more than it is in the interest of the commercial cities. The one thing essential to the prosperity and the hope and the growth of youth, whether a human being or a State, is the preservation of credit — credit is more necessary in new than in old communities. At present interest rates in the West and South are from 8 to 20 %, because of the doubt whether the creditor will have his fair share of the estate, if the debtor happens to be unfortunate. These communities pay the most fearful and unnecessary and exaggerated price for their resistance to this legislation.

Action on the bill was finally postponed by the Senate. With this defeat, five years elapsed before anyone was bold enough to bring forward another bankruptcy bill in Congress. At its Annual Meeting in 1887, however, the American Bar Association considered a report from its Committee on Commercial Law, which favored the adoption of the simple form of bill reported by Senator Ingalls in 1882, known as the Equity Bill. They said that it was only within the last few years that "anything like a serious and intelligent consideration of the subject had begun."

The agitation and discussion of this subject in a period of National prosperity is tantamount to the admission that, if a system shall be adopted at all, it will be because it is needed as a permanent institution for the regulation of the financial and commercial affairs of the country, and not merely to meet present and temporary difficulties.

With the year 1890, there began the eight years' struggle which finally resulted in the Bankrupt Law, enacted in 1898, and still existing (with many amendments). It was originally framed by a young lawyer of St. Louis, Jay L. Torrey, as a result of Conventions of National Commercial Organizations held in 1889 in St. Louis and in Minneapolis. Introduced in the House in 1890, in the 51st Congress with a Republican majority, it was passed after a two days' debate by a vote of 117 to 84, but was not acted on by the Senate. The chief opposition came from the Southerners, who said that the bill was not needed by farmers and that the demand for it "comes only from rich and powerful commercial corporations, wholesale dealers and boards of trade and associated jobbers." Charles A. Culbertson of Texas offered as a substitute a short bill providing only for voluntary bankruptcy; and such a bill undoubtedly met with favor in the West, for, from 1883 to 1889, a spirit of speculation had swept over the whole country west of the Missouri River, and lands had been purchased and farm mortgages given in enormous amount; the boom had now collapsed, property was depreciated and could not be sold, interest was defaulted, depression was rampant, and debtors cried out for relief.

In 1892 and 1893, in the 52d and 53d Congresses, the Torrey Bill, with amendments making it more lenient to debtors, was again introduced in Congress and exhaustively debated; but it was defeated in the House by a vote of 143 to 111 on December 8, 1893.[42] The Panic of 1893 was then in full blast; and the silver issue was becoming prominent. The Southern and Western Congressmen were almost unanimously opposed to any bill which provided for the collection of debts by creditors through a bankruptcy law, though some of them favored a purely voluntary bill for relief of debtors. William A. Stone of Pennsylvania said that "involuntary bankruptcy only brought about forced sales, and depreciated market values, injuring the whole country."

Such a bill should never be enacted when a business depression exists. The only argument for it is to afford greater facility to creditors in the collection of debts. If the approaching winter is severe, as many predict it will be, the State Legislatures will pass stay and extension laws. Either one policy or the other is wrong; my judgment is that the States are right. Indulgence to the debtor gives time and a breathing spell until more prosperous times arrive.

William J. Bryan agreed with him. Constantine B. Kilgore of Texas said that the bill was "vile and bad, subserving the interests of only a limited class of selfish people — the great wholesale merchants." Culbertson of Texas said that farmers' debts to retail merchants would be "dragged into the Bankruptcy Courts and their mortgages foreclosed with merciless promptness." The conditions of the time were vividly described by John Davis of Kansas, in a speech which might have been delivered last year. Most of the business failures, he said, had been due to contraction of the currency by the Government. He spoke of the general fall of prices, the prostration of agriculture, the depression of labor, the loss of peoples' houses by foreclosure of mortgage. "Our farmers are surrendering their homes into the hands of the Money Power. Our working people in the cities, mines, and factories and on the farms and railroads are suffering — merchants, bankrupt by the thousands annually. Farmers are unhoused and tenants evicted. Strikes of labor are rife on every hand. Men, women and children are crying for bread. Troops have recently been called out in four States at one time." William H. Denson of Alabama, in a vituperative speech, referred to the bill as "the most crushing and damnable instrumentality to oppress the farmers, laborers, debtors, or small dealers that the avarice, the greed, and the soulless cupidity of a Shylock could suggest . . . in this terrible, cruel, and destructive panic upon the country," and he said:

I raise my voice against this infernal engine of ruin, slavery, and destruction to the masses, another cruel and destructive instrumentality employed by the demon Money to crush out the farmers, the laborers and the masses of the country and make them subservient to and obedient slaves to the privileged classes, the capitalists, and Money Power of this land. I look upon it, in connection with the financial system now established and administered in this Union, as the last stroke necessary to destroy free institutions and drive home the last screw in the coffin of liberty.

Thomas R. Stockdale of Mississippi said:

The legislation of this country has already well-nigh bankrupted the farmers; and if we do not do something for their relief soon, it will be of little use to exempt them for they will have nothing. Farmers of the South have been obliged to mortgage their homesteads and then exempt property, with an exemption waiver clause. A merchant may want to carry the farmer through, but his creditor may force him into bankruptcy and pursue his former debtor.

William L. Terry of Arkansas said:

The present is no time for such a law, in the crash of falling values under the shadow of the advancing yellow standard — at a time when debtors are struggling to maintain their footing all over the land. The bill is another evidence of that vicious tendency of the times towards paternalism and centralization of power, and the constant effort to thrust the officious hand of law into the affairs of human life and supervise and regulate the business and conduct of men.

In retort to extravagant pleas of this kind, William J. Coombs of New York and many others protested "emphatically at persistent attempts made to array the debtor against the creditor classes." And Nelson Dingley, Jr., of Maine said:

There is no fixed class of debtors and creditors. The largest body of creditors are the working men, with savings in the banks. The largest debtors are men of means in large business operations, obliged constantly to hire money. Let us have done with this class talk about the money power and the poor man. Whatever weakens credit increases costs and raises rates of interest. The one thing that the South needs today is the confidence of men who have capital — the very men whom some of you stigmatize as the "money-power," "gold bugs," etc.

William C. Oates of Alabama (Democrat), who reported the bill, said:

137

This bill is intended not as a machine for the speedy collection of debts, but as an instrumentality on the one hand to relieve poor debtors from the burdens that would otherwise weigh them down, and on the other hand to furnish to creditors the means of reaching the property of the debtor and making an equitable distribution among honest creditors, in cases where the debtor is a rascal and is undertaking to conceal his property . . . or where the debtor in fact is insolvent. The definition of insolvency in this bill now differs from that of the Courts.

In opposing a purely voluntary bankruptcy bill offered by Joseph W. Bailey of Texas in behalf of the debtor class, Oates said that such a bill would ruin the credit of debtors, and that no bill should be passed constituting a privileged class.

Six months after the defeat of the general bill, Bailey, in July, 1894, again offered his voluntary bankruptcy bill, drafted on the simple lines of the Ingalls and Culbertson bills of ten years previous; and this bill was passed with a united Democratic support by a vote of 129 to 81. It applied to all debtors, both individuals and corporations (including National banks).[43] The Senate failed to act on the bill, as it was displaced by the bill for the free coinage of silver, pressed by Senator Jones of Arkansas.

In the next Congress, the Republicans having regained possession of the House, a much liberalized Torrey Bill was passed by a vote of 157 to 81, on May 2, 1896; and the House's previous action as to Bailey's voluntary bankruptcy bill was reversed by a vote of 113 to 129. The Senate, however, again failed to act. A strong appeal was made in the House by David B. Henderson of Iowa. From 1879 to 1895, he said, there had been 171,389 failures or one per cent of the total engaged in business; [44] and "in the terrible crash of 1893 and 1894 some of the best men in the country went down before the storm. Do we gain anything by keeping them there?" The bill specifically exempted farmers and wage earners. Again, however, it met with bitter opposition from Southern Congressmen who shared the views of David A. DeArmond of Missouri in saying:

> The only just ground for any bankrupt bill is to be found in the sad state of honest but insolvent debtors. Such legislation should be designed not necessarily or primarily to distribute their estates . . . but to give them relief. I deny that preferences are essentially and inevitably wrong. I think the principal, the sole just object of a bankrupt law should be the relief of the insolvent debtor.

And of William L. Terry of Arkansas, who said:

> This bill is another evidence of the grasping greed of the creditor classes of the North and the East reaching out to gather in and devour the substance of the debtors of the West and the South. This bill is wholly in interest of the wholesalers.

George F. Hoar in the Senate argued that the absence of any National bankruptcy law really worked in favor of creditors. Not only could they, by attachments and assignments, obtain preferences; but the debtors in many States had no State law under which they could get a discharge; and in no State could they be constitutionally discharged from debts due to outside creditors. He said: [45]

There are only 13 States having voluntary and involuntary bankruptcy laws. So that in 32 States the poor debtor has no hope, even if all his creditors dwell within the border of his own State. Then there are 10 States in addition which have the voluntary insolvent laws where the debtor can get relief from the debts contracted within his own State with citizens of his own State, if those debts were contracted after the passage of the law. Then there are 5 States of these which require the assent of a certain proportion of creditors, always, I believe, at least a majority in number and value. In some States, I think it is 2/3. So that in these 5 States, the debtor is dependent upon the will of the creditors.

The extent to which the advocates and opponents of bankruptcy legislation divided in sectional lines may be seen from the following figures of the House vote on the passage of the Torrey Bill on May 2, 1896:

Eastern States........	18 —	0, not voting	8
Middle States	49 —	4, " "	27
Southern States	28 —	39, " "	37
Western States	55 —	33, " "	40
Pacific States.........	7 —	5, " "	4
Totals	157 —	81, " "	116

In 1898, in the 55th Congress, the long struggle was ended by the enactment of the Torrey Bill, ("very much modified and changed," as Senator Hoar said). In the form presented by Senator Nelson of Minnesota, it passed the Senate on April 22, 1897, by a vote of 49 to 8; the House passed a more stringent bill on February 19, 1898, by a vote of 159 to 125; and after a long struggle in conference, the reformed bill passed the Senate and House on June 24 and 28, and was signed by President McKinley, July 1, 1898.[46]

The opposition to this measure, however, persisted with those who favored only voluntary bankruptcy; but during the debates amendments so to provide were defeated in both the Senate and the House. Oscar W. Underwood of Alabama stated in the House that "The only real sentiment in the country is for a voluntary bill to relieve those ruined by financial disasters in the last few years, due to repeal of the Bland-Allison Law and enactment of the Sherman Law and its repeal. Where is the man in the South or West who owned a farm, factory, or business house in 1890, that can get today more than fifty per cent of its then value?" Case Broderick of Kansas said that the demand in the West was for a voluntary bill:

There have been two unfortunate periods or conditions in that country which have tended to destroy the business interests and to bankrupt business men. One period perhaps was owing to misjudgment of the people, and the other was in no sense their fault but was their misfortune. From 1883 to 1889 a spirit of speculation swept over the entire country west of the Missouri River like a pestilence, and it unfortunately affected a large class of our people. They went wildly into speculation. They purchased more property than they had use for. They gave mortgages and incurred liabilities at the banks and when the boom collapsed, property was depreciated, people were in debt, mortgages had been given, interest had defaulted and there was no property which could be exchanged for money. This was the condition which prevailed in the country at that time. That was about 1889, and before the

141

people of the West had recovered from that condition which resulted in so much disaster, a panic came upon the country which spread all over it and paralyzed every interest. . . . The people of Kansas who survived the years of folly and disaster are now prosperous, but we want this bankruptcy measure to relieve those who were carried down by the current and lost.

Senator Stewart of Nevada said that "There never was a time when so many men in this country were unable to convert their property into money, although they have enough to pay their debts and more too as of to-day, but let a petition in bankruptcy be filed and a receiver be appointed and that is the end of them." And he engaged in an assault on the gold standard as increasing the load of debt payments of the great mass of the people. William D. Kelley of Pennsylvania stated that we must have voluntary bankruptcy so long as we had the gold standard, and he attacked the "curse of Clevelandism." Other Congressmen objected to the assumed fact that the bill applied to municipal corporations, though Hoar stated that it did not, as "they are agencies of sovereignty." Others termed it a bill demanded only by the great wholesale houses and leading jobbers, though Charles H. Grosvenor of Ohio pointed out that for many years Marshall, Field & Co. of Chicago and Claflin & Co. of New York had been strong opponents of the bill. James Gunn of Idaho alleged that in the distress due to repeal of the Sherman Law and the contraction of the currency, the bill was aimed at the West, in favor of the money loaning classes in the

East — also as a club to the South with its low price
of cotton. As David B. Henderson of Iowa said, the
"underlying spirit of most of the arguments against
the bill was sectionalism," but, said he, "credit is not
sectional, it is National. Morality knows no sections"; and he answered the sectional argument as
follows:

Those opposed are trying to create a sentiment against
such legislation in the West, by representing that it is in
the interest of the East alone and I believe some impression has been made by this argument. A more unjust
argument could not be used. It is wholly without foundation in fact. Why should the East be more interested?
The answer is made that when a debtor fails in the West,
the creditor there is nearer and can get in ahead of his
brother creditor in the East. This overlooks the fact of
Eastern creditors having collection agents or attorneys on
the spot and the facilities of the telegraph. The very argument is proof of the fact that the Western debtor is interested in having a law that will not make him the prey of
contending creditors, each trying to get the first grip at
the throat of the debtor, who is suspected of insolvency.

While the Act of 1898 has been frequently amended,
and violently criticised, it remains the law to-day,
after thirty-seven years. Efforts to repeal it, notably
in 1903, 1909, and 1910, have been made in Congress,
generally by Southern statesmen; and the old arguments have been repeated, that bankruptcy laws
should be for the relief of unfortunate debtors only,
and never for the provision of a new collecting
machinery. Such arguments, as before, have not
prevailed.[47]

143

By 1898, any questions of constitutionality which had been so earnestly debated in the past had entirely disappeared. Inclusion of corporations, extensions of bankruptcy to all classes of individual debtors, compositions, State exemptions of property — all were now fully recognized as within the Constitutional power of Congress. Moreover, it had become generally recognized that Congress should not exercise its power in the interest either of the debtor or of the creditor class alone — and that, in fact, there could be no such division of American citizens, since most of us are in one capacity debtors, and in another capacity creditors. There is now, therefore, a rather general acceptance of the principle that a bankruptcy law is required in the public interest of the Nation at large and for its welfare, apart from the effect of the law upon the particular individuals on whom it is to operate. Now, the chief interest of the Nation lies in the continuance of a man's business and the conservation of his property for the benefit of creditors and himself, and not in the sale and distribution of his assets among his creditors, or even in his own immediate discharge from his debts. Forced sale of property and stoppage of a business in times of depression constitute loss to the Nation at large, as well as to the individual debtors and creditors. Hence, in modern times, the belief has grown that the power of Congress to deal with "the subject of bankruptcies" cannot be confined merely to a law which shall collect, sell, and distribute a debtor's assets equally among his creditors. In the

144

past, those functions may have been deemed to be
the peculiar features of a bankruptcy law. Indeed,
it has been so stated by the Supreme Court.[48] But
they certainly cannot constitute the full extent to
which Congressional power may be exercised on the
general subject.

Fifty years ago, the Supreme Court, through Chief
Justice Waite, said as to composition agreements in a
bankruptcy law: "In no just sense do such governmental regulations deprive a person of his property
without due process of law. They simply require
each individual to conduct himself for the general
good so as not unnecessarily to injure another. . . .
Every member of a political community must necessarily part with some of the rights which, as an individual, not affected by his relations to others, he
might have retained. Such concessions make up the
consideration he gives for the obligation of the body
politic to protect him in life, liberty and property.
. . . Bankrupt laws, whatever may be the form they
assume, are of that character." [49] That was a very
broad view of the scope of a bankruptcy law. Under
it, certainly, Congress may, in its wise discretion, decide that the time has arrived in our economic and
social progress when, as between a debtor unable to
pay and a creditor unable to realize his full debt, it
is wiser for both and more beneficial to the Nation
that the Congressional power over the subject of
bankruptcies (or, in other words, over the inability
of a debtor to pay) should be exercised by providing
for the conservation of property equitably for cred-

itors through extension of time for payment and through reorganization of its debts, secured and unsecured. Such action by Congress is peculiarly consonant with legislation which has expressed the popular sentiment in the State throughout our history. It is a striking fact that, in spite of the Constitutional prohibition against laws impairing obligation of contract, whenever there has been any serious economic or financial upheaval in this country, the States have enacted stay-laws, that is, laws prolonging the period when a debtor's property should be exempt from execution, foreclosure, or suit, and giving to a debtor an interval in which to recuperate and obviate sale of his property at sacrifice prices in times of depression.[50] Court decisions holding such laws invalid have had little effect in preventing their enactment. All of which has been clear proof that American States preferred a policy of conservation and extension of time as a remedy, rather than collection of debts and discharge. It is true that State stay-laws, while temporarily helpful, have in the long run probably been injurious to the debtors by causing a loss of credit and confidence from creditors outside of the State; but had such a law been a National one, the effect might have been otherwise.

Undoubtedly, the enactment of such stay-laws by the States after the Revolution was one of the reasons for the adoption of the Contracts Clause in the Constitution. Yet, equally without doubt, the war, and trade, and other economic conditions from 1782 to 1787 (including especially the British debt situation) had made such stay-laws almost absolutely necessary, not only to aid debtors, but to preserve peace and economic and governmental stability in the States.[51] Thus, Virginia in 1783 suspended the issue of executions for a limited period. South Carolina in 1782, 1784, 1787, and 1788 passed various laws, staying suits, and in 1785 it passed its notorious "Pine-barrens Act," authorizing tender of land at two thirds of its appraised value or a stay if not accepted. Massachusetts in 1782 passed a similar act, authorizing a stay unless the creditor accepted in payment tender of cattle, timber, and other commodities. North Carolina in 1783 suspended all suits in Court temporarily. New Hampshire in 1785 provided for tender of land or personal property or a stay. It was because of the conditions giving rise to such legislation that Luther Martin in writing to the Maryland Legislature opposed the action of his co-framers of the Constitution, saying with considerable justice:[52]

I considered, sir, that there might be times of such great public calamities and distress, and of such extreme scarcity of specie, as should render it the duty of a government, for the preservation of even the most valuable part of its citizens, in some measure to interfere in their favor, by passing laws totally or partially stopping courts of justice; or authorizing the debtor to pay by installments, or by delivering up his property to his creditors at a reasonable and honest valuation. The times have been such as to render regulations of this kind necessary in *most* or *all* of the States, to prevent the wealthy creditor and the moneyed man from totally destroying the poor though industrious debtor. Such times may again arrive.

147

After the Constitution, the States continued to pass stay-laws, whenever business crises occurred. And it is to be noted that, while the State Courts usually held them invalid, such laws generally achieved their purpose of conserving the debtor's property and tiding him over, by reason of the fact that either the statute was not challenged in Court, or else the Court's decision was rendered after a considerable interval of time from the date of the statute. Thus, Virginia enacted in 1787 a law requiring judgment creditors to take property at three fourths of its appraised value and allowing replevin for twelve months after execution; and this law was in force until 1795 without test in the Court. In Pennsylvania, a stay-law of six and twelve months' duration was enacted in 1806, and its validity was never challenged. In Georgia, a stay-law passed in 1808 to aid debtors until the repeal of the Embargo Acts was upheld by the State Court;[53] a similar law existed in Maryland in 1808 and in Virginia in 1808, and another in 1814; Ohio passed an appraisal-law in 1809; North Carolina and Tennessee in 1809. All these laws were the result of embargo conditions. In North Carolina, a stay-law enacted in 1812 suspending judgment during the War of 1812 for a limited period upon giving of bond and security by the debtor was held invalid by the State Court, but not until the year 1814, when it had been in operation for two years.[54] In Louisiana, a stay-law of 1814 passed to meet war conditions was held valid in 1815.[55] In Tennessee, a law was enacted in 1819 to meet the serious financial conditions arising out of the crash of the State bank and providing for a stay of execution for two years unless the creditor would accept State notes in payment; it was held invalid by the State Court in 1821 after an interval of two years.[56] Illinois in 1819–1820 provided for stay unless creditors would accept bank notes in payment, and Ohio did likewise. Indiana had a stay-law in 1821 that was not tested in the Courts. In Missouri, a stay-law of 1821 passed to meet the financial crisis was held invalid by the State Court in 1822.[57] Kentucky enacted stay-, appraisal- and replevin-laws from 1819 to 1820 to meet the serious banking conditions; they were not held invalid until 1823 by the State Court.[58] In Mississippi, a stay-law of 1824 was held invalid by the State Court.[59] The flood of stay-and-appraisal-laws which followed the Panic of 1837 has been discussed *supra*.

The Civil War and Reconstruction produced in the Southern States another flood of stay-laws and of laws providing for exemption of property from execution, many of them of an extreme nature. A Southern jurist, writing in 1871, severely criticised them as follows: [60]

The legislatures of most of the Southern States have exercised uncontrollable discretion in passing Homestead and Exemption Laws . . . regardless of the effect on the rights of plaintiffs. It is contended that a great necessity existed, growing out of the war, which justified and sanctioned the violation of these great fundamental principles of government and constitutional law. But those who make this assertion should remember that creditors as

149

well as debtors suffered from the calamities of war. The rights of the former are entirely lost sight of in the general demoralization of society resulting from the evils of war, and in most of the Southern States the homestead and exemptions are so exorbitant and extravagant, that there are but few cases in which any property of the debtor is left, out of which creditors can procure their money. . . . There is but one remedy left, and that is, at an early day to test the constitutionality of these laws. . . . As the law now stands in most of the Southern States, no debts, whether simple debts or judgments, which were in existence before the passage of these laws, can be enforced. . . . Hence the only relief . . . is to be found before the Supreme Court of the United States.

While these laws were in most instances held invalid by the State Courts (and eventually by the United States Supreme Court), they largely achieved their purpose of giving temporary protection to the debtor and conservation of his property from forced sales, during the interval between enactment of the law and its invalidation by the Court. It was not until the year 1878, however, that the Supreme Court finally held all such laws unconstitutional, as, by changing the term of contract through postponement of time of payment and security of the judgment, the obligation of contract was held to be impaired "by making it less valuable to the creditor." [61] Among the State Courts holding the laws invalid, but only after a considerable interval during which the laws were in operation, were those of Texas acting in 1868 on stay-laws of 1861 and 1863; Mississippi acting in 1866 on stay-laws of 1861 and 1865; South Carolina acting in 1866 and 1868 on stay-laws of 1861, 1864, and 1865; Virginia acting in 1868 on stay-laws of 1861 and 1866; Alabama acting in 1867 on stay-laws of 1861; Florida acting in 1870 on a stay-law of 1861; North Carolina acting in 1869 on a stay-law of 1865–66, and 1868.[62] Other Southern State Courts held their stay-laws and exemption-laws constitutional; and as these cases were never carried to the United States Supreme Court, the laws continued in full operation until 1878, when that Court finally passed upon them.[63]

After the Panic of 1873, stay-laws were in force in nearly all the Western States, as John Sherman of Ohio stated in a debate in the Senate, February 3, 1874:

They have been uniformly enforced in nearly all Western States. . . where a man is sued and cannot pay. If he is willing to give security and show that he is willing and will be able to pay and has ability to secure the debt, he has a stay of exemption. Even where the debts are larger, the laws are so framed that a judgment cannot be taken except after a certain length of time after suit is brought. Means are given, in other words, to stay execution, sometimes with and sometimes without security.

O. H. P. Morton of Indiana also stated that the stay-laws in the Western States were usually for periods of six to twelve months, to enable debtors to sell property and pay debts without having their property sacrificed.[64]

The financial crisis of 1893 again produced stay-laws, especially in the West. A Kansas stay-law of 1893 allowing eighteen months redemption for real estate sold on execution or foreclosure was held invalid by the United States Supreme Court, but not until 1896.[65]

The present depression which began in 1929 has similarly resulted in the enactment of stay-laws or similar statutes in twenty-eight States. It is to be noted, however, that most of this legislation enacted in 1933 and 1934 was very speedily tested in the State Courts. In the United States Supreme Court a Minnesota moratorium law of 1933 was upheld in 1934 in a decision which broadened the power of the State to pass such laws and which modified the scope of the decisions rendered after the Panic of 1837.[66]

All these series of State statutes prove the long existing and prevailing sentiment of the country that, in time of financial distress, it was conservation and not sale and distribution of assets which was needed; and it is to be noted that, as long ago as 1882, it was recognized in Congress that a similar policy should be adopted in the exercise by Congress of its Bankruptcy Power. As early as 1882, Senator Ingalls inserted in his Equity Bankruptcy Bill provisions for stays and scaling down of indebtedness which may be regarded as the germ of the recent legislation of the past two years, and which have been overlooked by those who claim that the recent statutes are entirely novel. Novel they may be, in their precise detail, but not in principle. Ingalls' bill in 1882 contained the following provision (and he did not originate it, for the Louisiana State insolvency law contained a similar provision): [67]

Sec. 3. That the Court shall have power to grant extensions of time for payment, and to reduce the amount of indebtedness pro rata, for the purpose of allowing the debtor to proceed with his business, if it shall seem best to do so. And any agreement between the debtor and a majority in amount and number of his creditors may be carried into effect if approved by the Court.

Sec. 4. The Court may, at any time during the proceedings, order that all or any other proceedings be stayed or dismissed, and may require all or any claims to be presented to it for determination, or may allow any other proceeding to be prosecuted to final judgment; and such judgment to be filed in bankruptcy. And any claim not due may be matured by a rebate under an order of the Court.

He explained its purpose as follows:

This provision is designed to prevent the business of bankrupt wreckers and to preserve the entire estate for the creditors and their customers in whose success they are immediately interested. It would prevent the destruction through the malice or ill will of a rival in trade or a personal enemy of a business worth preserving. The good will of an established business may be worth more, as a means of acquiring money for the payment of liabilities, than the goods in the factory or store. In many cases, a mere extension of time would enable the debtor to realize funds and make payment in full. In other cases, a reduction of 25 % or 50 % of the liabilities would enable him to pay the remaining 50 % or 75 % when under a forced commission in bankruptcy, the creditors might realize but a fraction of that amount. The design of this is to prevent bankruptcies. It is remedial and beneficent. One great difficulty in all bankruptcy systems has been the absence of conservative provisions. They could do nothing to protect or to aid, but they were potent to destroy. . . . In all cases it is to the interest, both of the public, and of the creditors, to have the merchant or manufacturer go on with his business if he can. And if he has acted honestly, he should be allowed to summon his creditors, state his case to the Court, show his good faith, fair dealing, and freedom from fraud, the ratio of his assets to his liabilities, and have his indebtedness reduced by an order of the Court to that percentage which will enable him to go on in business, meeting the new obligations in full. . . . In the other class of failures arising chiefly in time of financial panic, or accident such as fire, wreck, etc., the suspension of payments may not arise from any inadequacy of assets but solely from inability to realize immediate cash. To destroy a business house and wreck the fortune of an upright and able business man, under such circumstances where he has an abundance of assets to meet every obligation, would seem an act of wantonness such as ought not to be tolerated under an enlightened system of jurisprudence. . . . So I think, as of the highest importance in a bankruptcy law, such provisions for reducing liabilities pro rata and for granting extensions of time of payments.

It is apparently in consonance with these views and the constantly expanding conception of the scope of the Bankruptcy Power under the Constitution, held both by Congress and by the Supreme Court, that the recent bankruptcy legislation has been enacted.[68] In upholding, on April 1, 1935, the validity of the Railroad Reorganization Act of 1933 (which appended a new Section 77 to the existing Bankruptcy Act), Justice Sutherland has said: "From the beginning, the tendency of legislation and of judicial interpretation has been uniformly in the direction of progressive liberalization in respect of the operation of the bankruptcy power"; and after citing the ad-

vanced steps taken by the voluntary bankruptcy and
by the composition statutes, he stated:

> The fundamental and radically progressive nature of
> these extensions becomes apparent upon their mere state-
> ment; but all have been judicially approved or accepted
> as falling within the power conferred by the bankruptcy
> clause of the Constitution. Taken altogether, they demon-
> strate in a very striking way the capacity of the bankruptcy
> clause to meet new conditions as they have been disclosed
> as a result of the tremendous growth of business and devel-
> opment of human activities from 1800 to the present day.
> And these acts, far-reaching though they may be, have not
> gone beyond the limit of congressional power; but rather
> have constituted extensions into a field whose boundaries
> may not yet be fully revealed. . . . A railway is a unit; it
> cannot be divided up and disposed of piecemeal like a stock
> of goods. It must be sold, if sold at all, as a unit and as a
> going concern. Its activities cannot be halted because its
> continuous, uninterrupted operation is necessary in the
> public interest; and for the preservation of that interest,
> as well as for the protection of the various private interests
> involved, reorganization was evidently regarded as the
> most feasible solution whenever the corporation had be-
> come "insolvent or unable to meet its debts as they
> mature."

With respect to the power of Congress under the
Bankruptcy Clause to affect the rights of a secured
creditor, the Supreme Court has set a limit in the
recent decision in the *Radford Case* on May 27, 1935,
holding the Frazier-Lemke Act of June 28, 1934,
unconstitutional.[69] In that case, legislative provisions
taking from a mortgagee certain existing rights and
vesting in the mortgagor certain rights in the mort-

gaged property not possessed by him before were held invalid, as depriving the mortgagee of his property without due process of law. The Bankruptcy Power, said the Court, was limited by the Fifth Amendment. Justice Brandeis stated:

It is true that the position of a secured creditor, who has rights in specific property, differs fundamentally from that of an unsecured creditor, who has none; and that the Frazier-Lemke Act is the first instance of an attempt, by a bankruptcy act, to abridge, *solely in the interest of the mortgagor*, a substantive right of the mortgagee in specific property held as security. But we have no occasion to decide in this case whether the bankruptcy clause confers upon Congress generally the power to abridge the mortgagee's rights in specific property. Paragraph 7 declares that "the provisions of this act shall apply only to debts existing at the time this act becomes effective." The power over property pledged as security after the date of the act may be greater than over property pledged before; and this act deals only with preexisting mortgages. Because the act is retroactive in terms and as here applied purports to take away rights of the mortgagee in specific property, another provision of the Constitution is controlling. [Italics mine.]

The very extreme provisions of this statute undoubtedly warranted the decision. But there still may be a doubt whether *every* retroactive interference with a creditor's rights is rendered impossible, under this decision.[70] For retroactive action has been an essential part of the Bankruptcy Power in the past, and one of the chief reasons for the enactment of bankruptcy laws has been to wipe out debts existing at the date of such enactment. Since the Court has long held that the grant of the Bankruptcy Power to Congress involves the power to impair the obligation of contracts, it is difficult to see why the contract of a secured creditor may not be impaired as well as the contract of an unsecured creditor.[71] It would appear that a statute which prevents A from suing on B's unsecured note takes away property rights belonging to A as well as discharges B's personal obligation. To the extent that it deprives A of a property right of suit which he had in the past, it is retroactive in the same manner as a statute which takes away property held by A under B's secured note. In both cases, it would seem that the statute was retroactive as to a property right of A. If Congress may abolish the entire indebtedness of B to A on B's unsecured note, is it entirely without power to affect the indebtedness of B to A on B's secured note? Is it without power to reduce such indebtedness, on equitable terms under the Bankruptcy Clause? Certainly the Railroad Reorganization Act of 1934 (which the Court has upheld) interfered with pre-existing rights of secured creditors.[72] It is to be noted that in the Radford Case, the abridgment of the creditor's rights made by the statute was stated by the Court to be *"solely in the interest of the mortgagor."* If the abridgement had been or should be made *in the interest of all parties concerned, creditors, debtors, and the general public,* would the mere fact that it affected retroactively prior existing rights of a creditor render it invalid under the Fifth Amendment? There may at least be room for doubt.

Probably, Congress, under the Bankruptcy Clause, may enact a National stay-law or moratorium-law which would postpone payment of a debt or affect the remedy for its collection, to the same extent that a State Legislature could act under the State police power; and since the Bankruptcy Clause allows Congress to impair contracts, while the States are forbidden so to do, it is possible that the power of Congress to pass stay-law legislation is broader than the power of the States.[73]

However objectionable the Frazier-Lemke Act may have been under the Fifth Amendment, because of its effect in depriving the creditor of his rights for the sole benefit of the debtor, it still remains true that, in general, rights of both creditors and debtors must be subject to the power of Congress to act for the National interest under the Bankruptcy Clause. For, as William P. Fessenden said, in 1841:

The power of Government to pass laws affecting the obligation of contracts is derived from the nature of the Government itself. . . . It is a necessary power; for it is by no means difficult to imagine a condition of things in which the safety and well being of the Nation would imperatively demand its exercise. Take the case, for example, in which a whole community becomes insolvent by some stupendous accident, or by some magnificent but fallacious scheme, such as other countries have seen and felt at no distant day. Can it be pretended that a power to apply a remedy to a disorder that is paralyzing and destroying the body politic exists nowhere? Such an idea is a libel upon the very name of Government. And yet if we have not this power, it exists nowhere in this country. It is yielded up by the States. . . . As a general rule, the obligation of contracts should be held inviolable. Regard should always be had to the interests and rights of the citizens. But those rights and those interests must yield to high considerations of public policy. They must necessarily be made subservient to the good of the State.

And so in viewing the possibilities of Constitutional power under the Bankruptcy Clause, we really come back to what Henry Clay said, April 4, 1840:

The right of the State (Nation) to the use of the unimpaired faculties of its citizens as producers, as consumers, and as defenders of the Commonwealth, is paramount to any rights or relations which can be created between citizen and citizen. . . . I maintain that the public right of the State (Nation) in all the faculties of its members, moral and physical, is paramount to any supposed rights which appertain to a private creditor. This is the great principle which lies at the bottom of all bankrupt laws.

It is this principle which was embodied in the Bankruptcy Clause of the Constitution, and to give effect to which, in the changing conditions in our economic history, the Constitution has hitherto always been found entirely adequate.

NOTES

NOTES TO PART I

1. Taney, C. J., in *Aldredge v. Williams* (1845) 3 Howard 1, 24: "In expounding this law, the judgment of the Court cannot, in any degree, be influenced by the construction placed upon it by individual members of Congress in the debates which took place on its passage, nor by the motives or reasons assigned by them for supporting or opposing amendments that were offered." Cf. Story, J. in *Mitchell v. Great Work etc. Co.* (1843) 2 Story 648, F. C. 9663. Bronson, J. in *Sackett v. Andrews* (1843) 5 Hill 327, said: "I must be permitted to add that a legislative debate in modern times proves very little on any subject." And see cases cited in *U. S. Supreme Court Reports Digest* (1929) VIII, 5792–5793.
2. *Sawyer v. Hoag* (1873) 17 Wall. 610.
3. *19th Cong., 1st Sess.*, speech of Robert Y. Hayne, March 4, 1826.
4. *Messages and State Papers of the Confederacy* (1900), by John D. Richardson, I, 42.
5. See for full outline of these statutes, *A History of the Bankruptcy Clause of the United States of America* (1916), by F. Regis Noel. For an account of early Colonial and State laws on the subject, see *Commentaries on the Constitution*, by Joseph Story, II, Sections 1106–1113; "Bankruptcy or Commercial Regulation," by James R. Olmstead, *Harv. Law Rev.* (1902) XV; "Is Section 77 B a proper Part of a Bankruptcy Act?" by J. J. Kaplan, *Amer. Bar Ass. Journal* (1935) XXXI.

   For an account of prior bankruptcy laws in England, see "The Early History of English Bankruptcy" (1919), *Univ. of Penn. Law Rev.* LXXI; *Report of the Solicitor General of the United States* in *72d Cong., 1st Sess.*, Senate Document No. 65; *Remington on Bankruptcy* (4th Ed.) 1–13.
6. *39th Cong., 2d Sess.*, in the Senate, speech of Thomas A. Jenckes of Rhode Island (p. 2472).
7. Madison in his *Preface to Debates in the Convention*, in describing the weaknesses of the old Confederation, said: "Among the defects which had been severely felt was the want of uniformity in cases requiring it, as laws of naturali-

163

zation and bankruptcy." The date of this Madison draft was between 1830 and 1836; see *The Debates in the Federal Convention of 1787* (ed. by Gaillard Hunt and James Brown Scott, 1920) 1, note 2.

In the Pennsylvania State Convention, Thomas McKean stated that "the power of Congress to regulate trade, to establish a general rule of naturalization, and to enact uniform laws of bankruptcies is not objected to." *Pennsylvania and the Federal Constitution, 1787–1788* (1888), by John Bach McMaster and Frederick D. Stone, 421.

8. *25th Cong., 1st Sess.*, in the Senate, speech of Thomas H. Benton, October 12, 1837; "Bankruptcy and Commercial Regulation," by James M. Olmstead, *Harv. Law Rev.* (June, 1902) xv, 829; see esp. *Bankruptcy. A Study in Comparative Legislation* (1893), by A. Whitney Dunscomb, Jr.

9. *Harv. Law Rev., supra*, xv, 834–835.

10. "The Corporate Reorganization Provision in Senate Bill 3866," by B. M., *Yale Law Journal* (1932) XLII, 387 et seq.

11. *Writings of Thomas Jefferson* (Ford Ed.) VI, letters to James Monroe, July 10, 1791; Edward Rutledge, August 29, 1791; Plumard de Rieux, January 6, 1792; Thomas Mann Randolph, March 16, April 19, 1792; William Short, March 18, 1792; David Humphreys, April 9, 1792; Francis Eppes, April 14, 1792. See also *History of the People of the United States*, by John Bach McMaster, II, 22–23, 38–42, 80–82.

12. *2d Cong., 1st Sess.*, November 9, 1791; *2d Cong., 2d Sess.*, November 21, December 6, 1792; *3d Cong., 1st Sess.*, December 13, 1793; *3d Cong., 2d Sess.*, December 9, 1794; *4th Cong., 1st Sess.*, December 16, 1795, January 13, 1796; *4th Cong., 2d Sess.*, December 29, 1796 — all in the House of Representatives.

13. See *The Great American Land Bubble* (1932), by A. M. Sokolski, 35–53.

14. *5th Cong., 2d Sess.*, November 27, 1797, January 1, 1798; *5th Cong., 3d Sess.*, December 11, 14, 20, 26, 1798, January 1, 2, 8, 9, 14, 15, 1799.

15. *5th Cong., 2d Sess.*, January 6, 1799.

16. As to this, James A. Bayard said, February 18, 1803, *7th Cong., 2d Sess.*, in the House: "One great use of a bankrupt system is its exposing landed property to sale for payment

of debts, as it is my conviction that no country can be commercial where land is not answerable for the payment*of debts. Exemption of lands is a remnant of feudal policy and ought to be consigned to the same tomb with its other trappings. . . . Unquestionable defects exist in the law."

17. *Writings of Thomas Jefferson* (Ford Ed.) vii, 193–194, 196, 198, letters to Thomas Mann Randolph, December 21, 1792, and to John Francis Mercer, December 19, 1792; "Notes on Bankrupt Bill, December 1792," *ibid.*, vii.

18. Bayard wrote to Richard Bassett, February 1, 1800: "For some days past, we have been labouring very hard to carry thro the House our Bankrupt Bill. The Antis have discovered that it will add strength to the federal compact and they make every exertion to defeat it. It had like to have been lost upon the question of engrossing. It was kept alive by the casting vote of the Speaker (T. Sedgwick) tho Nicholas (John) (who will never forgive himself for the blunder) voted with us thro civility. Since then we have been obliged to intrigue and negotiate, in order to gain strength and we have not been without success. Accommodation has been the worst instrument we have made use of. Gentlemen have been indulged with amendments which have half spoiled the Bill. But we have determined to have it, upon any terms we can get it." *Amer. Hist. Ass. Report, 1913*, ii, "Papers of James A. Bayard."

19. *6th Cong., 1st Sess.*, in the House, January 6, 21, February 11, 21, 1800; in the Senate, March 17, 20, 28, 1800. The Act of April 4, 1800 (2 Stat. 19–36), containing 64 sections, applied to "any merchant or other person residing within the United States, actually using the trade of merchandise, by buying and selling in gross, or by retail, or dealing in exchange or as a banker, broker, factor, underwriter, or marine insurer."

Robert G. Harper wrote to his constituents, May 15, 1800, "Papers of James A. Bayard," in *Amer. Hist. Ass. Report, 1913*, ii, 101–102: "Among the most important laws of the session thus terminated, viz., the Bankrupt Act which has long been an object of attention in Congress, but hitherto delayed by the difficulty and extent of this subject itself, or by the pressure of matters more immediately interesting. Its operation is confined to merchants and dealers, and will be rarely felt except in the great commercial towns; for a person must owe at least a thousand dollars before it can affect him. Its object is, in the first place, to support mercantile credit, by protecting the rights of creditors against the fraud of dishonest and the folly of imprudent debtors who may waste or conceal their property while the ordinary forms of law are going on against them; and secondly to encourage fair industry and prudent conduct, by enabling honest debtors reduced by misfortune, to give up their property, free themselves entirely from their debts, and begin the world anew, which no man will ever have the courage to do, while a load of old debts is hanging on him. A system so new, so extensive, and operating on such a variety of unseen cases, will, no doubt, be found very imperfect at first, and in need of frequent revision and amendment according to the light which experience alone can afford. It may also be liable to abuse in many instances, for what human institution may not be perverted? But the example of other countries proves that to a trading people a bankrupt law is highly beneficial if not absolutely necessary."

20. *Writings of Thomas Jefferson* (Ford Ed.) ix, 112, 120, letter to James Madison, March 4, 1800. To Thomas Mann Randolph, Jefferson wrote, February 2, 1800: "I was mistaken last week in saying no more failures had happened. New ones have been declaring every day in Baltimore, others here and at New York. The last here have been Nottnagil, Montmollin & Co. and Peter Blight. These sums are enormous. I do not know the firms of the bankrupt houses in Baltimore but the crash will be incalculable. In the present stagnation of commerce and particularly that in tobacco, it is difficult to transfer money from hence to Richmond."

21. *7th Cong., 2d Sess.*, in the House, January 13, February 16, 18, 1803; a motion to postpone the consideration of a Committee Report as to the inadvisability of repeal was carried by a vote of 50 to 39.

22. *8th Cong., 1st Sess.*, in the Senate, December 13, 1803; in the House, November 23, 28, 1803.

John Sergeant of Pennsylvania said in the House, December 11, 1821, that the Act of 1800 "was passed at a time of as great party excitement as ever existed in the United States;

it made its appearance in the midst of the ferment occasioned by other measures and is never thought of by many without associating it in idea with other measures of that day."

Robert Wright of Maryland stated in the House, March 6, 1822, that he was in the Senate at the time of the repeal, that it was a partisan act due to the high state of party which then prevailed. Andrew Stevenson of Virginia on the contrary stated, January 23, 1822, that if the Act of 1800 had been regarded as a party measure, it would have been expunged during the earliest acts of the new Administration, but that the Act of 1800 "was passed from other and better motives, as an experiment called for at that time by the commercial part of the community and which expired under the weight of its own sins." So too Joseph Hemphill of Pennsylvania said, February 11, 1822, that it was "clearly a mistake to say that the Act was considered of a political nature by Jefferson's party." *17th Cong., 1st Sess.*

23. See speech of John Holmes of Massachusetts in the House, February 17, 1817, *15th Cong., 1st Sess.* Edwin C. Brandenburg in his *Law of Bankruptcy* (1898) 4, states the reason for repeal as follows (somewhat erroneously, since pressure for repeal came from the creditor class): "The fact that it was intended chiefly for the protection of creditors, the sparseness of the settlements, the scarcity of Federal Courts, and the difficulty and slowness of travel, contributed mainly to its failure. The distance between places where courts were held, by reason of the method of locomotion, made ready relief almost impossible and soon brought about a demand for the repeal of the law."

See speech of Joseph Hopkinson of Pennsylvania in the House, February 20, 1818, *15th Cong., 1st Sess.*: "Our country grew extravagantly and suddenly rich by the aggregate of commercial exertions, while individuals were daily falling into ruin by the unexpected Orders and Decrees and the unauthorized violence of belligerents. In 1800, there had accumulated a vast mass of insolvent debtors who had previously been stripped of every cent. . . . The public saw hundreds of men obtaining a discharge who surrendered little or nothing to their creditors. . . . They saw too that in almost all the cases the commission was evidently taken out at the instance of the bankrupt himself though pretending to be a proceeding of the creditor against the bankrupt. Can we wonder then that the public should exclaim, if this is the effect of a bankrupt law, it is really intended only for the debtor and affords nothing to the creditor?"

24. President Monroe submitted the figures to Congress in 1822, showing the number of bankruptcy proceedings under the Act of 1800, as follows: 208 in Pennsylvania, 166 in New York, 58 in Maryland, 45 in Virginia, 14 in the District of Columbia, figures for the other States not being given. *17th Cong., 1st Sess.*, January 4, 8, 31, 1822.

25. See *In re Robert Morris*, F. C. 9825 in the United District Court of Pennsylvania, in February, 1837; his commission of bankruptcy issued July 28, 1801, and only a portion (90) of his creditors proved their claims, for $3,000,000.

26. Thomas Cooper, while in prison in Philadelphia, under sentence for violation of the Sedition Act of 1798 wrote a book on *The Bankrupt Law of America, Compared with the Bankrupt Law of England,* published in 1801 (the copy in the Library of Congress being inscribed "With the Author's respects to Thomas Jefferson, Pres. of the U. States"). In his preface, he said: "The bankrupt system is new in this country; its defects are very many, far more than I have touched upon — so many as to induce a doubt from the Bench whether it had not done more harm than good in England. Some few of these defects we have remedied. Most of them we have retained. . . . As this book is intended for a country where the law may be considered as an experiment, I hope the liberty I have taken will not be deemed too great."

Joseph Story in his *Commentaries on the Constitution* said in 1830: "One of the most pressing grievances bearing upon commercial, manufacturing, and agricultural interests at the present moment is the total want of a general system of bankruptcy. It is well known that the power has lain dormant except for a short period ever since the Constitution was adopted; and the excellent system they put into operation was repealed before it had any fair trial, upon grounds generally believed to be wholly beside its merits and from causes more easily understood than deliberately vindicated."

27. See speech of Thomas R. Mitchell of South Carolina in the House, February 12, 1822, *17th Cong.*, *1st Sess.* See also *Financial History of the United States from 1789 to 1860* (1883), by Albert S. Bolles, 85: "It may be remarked that besides the protection thrown over the manufacturing interest by Congress during this period, the wars which raged in Europe produced a favorable effect. American commerce rode the waves of an unexampled and brilliant prosperity. As the United States was a neutral nation, she fattened on the miseries of the European nations and her commerce increased with astonishing rapidity. . . . Our manufacturers flourished from the same cause, though not to a corresponding degree with our commerce."

28. *11th Cong.*, *1st Sess.*, in the House, December 6, 1809; *12th Cong.*, *1st Sess.*, in the House, January 1, 1812, when a motion for a Committee to inquire into the expediency of a bankruptcy law was lost by a vote of 50 to 86.

29. *Golden v. Prince* (April, 1814) 3 Wash. C. C. 313; 5 Hall L. J. 502; F. C. 5509. The Pennsylvania law in question had been enacted March 13, 1812, applied only to Philadelphia, and had been repealed December 21, 1812.

30. *13th Cong.*, *2d Sess.*, in the House, December 12, 1814; see bill reported by Charles J. Ingersoll of Pennsylvania from the Judiciary Committee, January 3, 1815.

31. *14th Cong.*, *1st Sess.*, in the House, January 4, February 27, April 27, 1816. The Governors of Louisiana and of Rhode Island in 1816 urged bankruptcy legislation by Congress.

32. *15th Cong.*, *1st Sess.*, in the House, December 12, 1817, February 13, 16, 17, 18, 19, 20, 24, 25, 1818; see also *15th Cong.*, *2d Sess.*, November 24, 1818, when Hopkinson again reported his bill.

33. *McMillan v. McNeil* (1819) 4 Wheaton 209; see comment on the Reporter's statement, made by Washington, J. in *Ogden v. Saunders* (1827) 12 Wheaton, p. 255, and by Johnson, J., *ibid.*, p. 272. See also attack on the McMillan decision by Holmes of Maine in the Senate, February 8, 1821, *16th Cong.*, *2d Sess.*, and as late as January 27, 1827, *19th Cong.*, *2d Sess.*, Elias Kent Kane of Illinois said in the Senate that under that decision no power remained in the States to discharge debtors.

BANKRUPTCY IN UNITED STATES HISTORY

34. See *Smith v. Mead* (1820) 3 Conn. 253; *Boardman v. Deforest* (1823) 5 Conn. 1. In *Mather v. Bush* (1819) 16 John. 246, and *Blanchard v. Russell* (1816) 13 Mass., a contrary view was held.
35. See *The Supreme Court in United States History* (Rev. Ed. 1926), by Charles Warren, I, 493–498.
36. *16th Cong., 2d Sess.*, in the Senate, February 7, 1821.
37. *15th Cong., 1st Sess.*, in the House, speech of Philip P. Barbour of Virginia, February 25, 1818; *27th Cong., 1st Sess.*, in the Senate, July 25, 1841, App. p. 205. And as Senator Otis of Massachusetts said in the Senate (*16th Cong., 2d Sess.*, February 7, 1821): "In what country, and at what period has commerce been exposed to the tremendous, sudden, and total vicissitudes which it has undergone in our nation and in our time? . . . In many parts of the country an unsound currency has supplanted a valuable medium, and the depreciation of capital in land, produce, ships, and merchandise is universal. No reliance can be placed on the foreign or domestic market, and the want of confidence has caused the previous metals to be withdrawn from circulation, and to be hoarded in the coffers of the rich."
See also "The Depression of 1819–1822. A Social History," by Samuel Rezneck, *Amer. Hist. Rev.* (1933), XXXIX.
38. Judge Joseph Story wrote to Stephen White, February 27, 1820: "The Bankrupt Bill will not be passed this season. So much time is wasted that there is no chance for melioration of our code of laws upon this or indeed upon any other subject. There are many enemies of a Bankrupt system, some friends, and many very lukewarm or indifferent. I despair of any great public measure founded on national policy." Story wrote to W. Pettyplace, February 28, 1821: "I begin to believe the bill will pass and without amendments (in the House). If amended, it will be lost; and therefore the friends of the bill will resist every attempt to amend. There is a great excitement on the subject. Mr. Clay has behaved nobly; he delivered in the course of this day a most eloquent, pathetic, and manly speech in its favor; he deserves infinite credit as, but for his exertions, the bill would be inevitably lost. It is generally now believed that the bill will pass, though its enemies will make every possible effort

170

to defeat it. The scene of this day was a small specimen of what will doubtless take place. It was truly undignified, not to say tumultous. The House did not adjourn till about half past seven o'clock." *Life and Letters of Joseph Story* (1851) I, 382, 396.

39. *16th Cong., 1st Sess.*, in the Senate, January 12, 21, March 10, 13, 16, 17, 20, 21, 22, 27, 30, 1820; *16th Cong., 2d Sess.*, in the Senate, January 9, 11, 16, February 6, 7, 8, 12, 13, 14, 15, 20, 1821; in the House, February 21, 1821, bill reported by John Sergeant of Pennsylvania and laid on the table.

40. *17th Cong., 1st Sess.*, in the House, December 11, 1821, January 21, 22, 23, 25, February 7, 8, 11, 12, 14, 15, 16, 18, 19, 21, March 6, 8, 9, 10, 12, 1822. An adverse report was tabled in the *18th Cong., 1st Sess.*, in the House, December 30, 1823, and see resolution by Daniel Webster favoring a law in the future, May 26, 1824. See *Memoirs of John Quincy Adams* IV, 325, 498, V, 128 et seq.

41. *New York Statesman*, March 15, 1822.

42. *Essay on a National Bankrupt Law* (December, 1825), by Ralph I. Lockwood, and see his table of votes on the bill arranged by States.

43. See *16th Cong., 2d Sess.*, in the Senate, speeches of Jonathan Roberts of Pennsylvania, February 6, 1821, and John Holmes of Maine, February 8, 1821; motion of Walter Lowrie of Pennsylvania, February 13, 1821. *17th Cong., 1st Sess.*, in the House, Alexander Stevenson of Virginia, January 23, 1821; A. Smyth of Virginia, January 25, 1821; William S. Archer of Virginia, February 13, 1822; Philip P. Barbour of Virginia, February 15, 1822; James Buchanan of Pennsylvania, March 12, 1822. See speeches in favor of the Constitutional power by H. G. Otis of Massachusetts, in the Senate, February 7, 1821; and in the House by Joseph Hemphill of Pennsylvania, February 11, 1822.

44. *17th Cong., 1st Sess.*, in the House, February 11, 1822.

45. *17th Cong., 1st Sess.*, in the House, March 6, 1822.

46. *Essay on A National Bankrupt Law* (December, 1825), by Ralph I. Lockwood.

47. *17th Cong., 1st Sess.*, in the House, January 23, 1822.

48. *17th Cong., 1st Sess.*, speeches of Lemuel Sawyer of North Carolina, February 16, 1822; James Buchanan, March 22,

1822, stated that in Rhode Island real estate could not be reached by a creditor.

49. *15th Cong., 1st Sess.*, in the House, speeches of Samuel Smith of Maryland, February 18, 1818; Joseph Hopkinson, February 20, 1818; *19th Cong., 1st Sess.*, in the Senate, John McPherson Berrien of Georgia, May 24, 1826.

50. *17th Cong., 1st Sess.*, February 14, 1822.

51. Thomas Jefferson wrote to James Pleasants, *Writings of Thomas Jefferson* (Ford Ed.) XII, December 26, 1821: "I find you are to be harassed again with a bankrupt law. Could you not compromise between agriculture and commerce, by passing such a law which like the bylaws of incorporate towns should be binding on the inhabitants of such towns only, being the residence of commerce, leaving the agriculturists, inhabitants of the country, in undisturbed possession of the rights and modes of proceedings to which their habits, their interests and their partialities attach them? This would be as *uniform* as other laws of local obligation."

52. *15th Cong., 1st Sess.*, in the House, speeches of John Tyler of Virginia, February 17, 1818; John Hopkinson of Pennsylvania, February 20, 1818.

53. *15th Cong., 1st Sess.*, in the House, February 25, 1818.

54. *17th Cong., 1st Sess.*, in the House, February 11, 1822.

55. *15th Cong., 1st Sess.*, in the House, February 17, 1818.

56. *15th Cong., 1st Sess.*, see for instance, speech of Elijah H. Mills of Massachusetts in the House, February 19, 1818; *17th Cong., 1st Sess.*, in the House, speech of Samuel H. Woodson of Kentucky, February 21, 1822.

57. *16th Cong., 2d Sess.*, in the Senate, February 7, 1821.

58. *18th Cong., 1st Sess.*, in the House, May 26, 1824. Judge Story wrote to Webster, January 4, 1824 (Story, I, 437): "What hope of a Bankrupt Act? Why will you not ask me to put one into the shape of a code of articles? I want to try my hand at codifying a Bankrupt ordinance."

59. Hayne pointed out in his speech of May 1, 1826, that the Senate had voted for a form of voluntary bankruptcy, March 23, 1820, by 25 to 13, and March 31, 1820, by 25 to 16.

60. *19th Cong., 1st Sess.*, December 9, 13, 1825, February 21,
    April 28, May 1, 3, 4, 1826 (the Senate adjourning May 20,
    1826).
    President John Quincy Adams, in his Message of Decem-
    ber 6, 1825, had recommended the passage of a bankruptcy
    law, as "an object of deepest interest to society."
61. This section, taken from the British statute of 6 Geo. IV,
    c. XVI, ss. 133–134, was described by Samuel Sewall in
    an article "On a National Bankrupt Law" in *American
    Jurist* (January, 1829) I, 35, as follows: "This arrange-
    ment will often enable the debtor by resuming his business
    to manage his property to greater advantage than any as-
    signee could do, besides relieving it from many expenses —
    also advantageous to creditors in many instances by giving
    them negotiable paper with good names which will be imme-
    diately available in the money market, instead of an uncer-
    tain claim against a bankrupt estate from which nothing
    may be realized for a long period."
62. *19th Cong., 2d Sess.*, in the Senate, December 6, 28, January
    18, 23, 24, 26, 29, 31, February 1, 2, 6, 1827.

NOTES TO PART II

1. *Life and Letters of Joseph Story* (1851) I, letter of February 4, 1827.

2. *19th Cong., 2d Sess.*, speeches of John McKinley of Alabama, in the Senate, January 24, 1827; Martin Van Buren of New York, in the Senate, January 23, 1827.

3. *The Supreme Court in United States History* (Rev. Ed. 1926), by Charles Warren, II, 687. *Ogden v. Saunders* was filed in Louisiana in the United States District Court, May 14, 1814, and in the Supreme Court, February 5, 1820.

4. Webster wrote to Mason, February 15: "Nothing has yet been done with the B[ill] and it seems too late to do anything. The question is before the Court whether the State bankruptcy laws are valid. The general opinion is that the six Judges now here will be equally divided on the point. I confess, however, I have a strong suspicion there will be an opinion and that that opinion will be against the State laws. If there were time remaining the decision, should it happen, might help the Bill."

5. See criticism of this decision by Woodbury, J. in *Taine v. Smith* (1846); and see "Has a State the Power to Discharge a Debt Due to a Non Resident," by Conrad Reno, *Amer. Law Rev.* (1898) XXXII; "Ogden v. Saunders Reviewed," by Conrad Reno, *Amer. Law Register* (1888) XXXVI; "A Discharge in Insolvency and Its Effect on Non Residents," by Hollis R. Bailey, *Harv. Law Rev.* (1893) VI.

   As early as 1811, Washington, J. had made a similar decision, see *Green v. Sarmiento*, 3 Wash. C. C. 17, and he also cited the case of *Bank v. Greenleaf* decided "in the Circuit Court in Virginia, ten or twelve years ago."

6. See *The Supreme Court in United States History* (Rev. Ed. 1926), by Charles Warren, I, 689–690.

7. "On a National Bankrupt Law," by Samuel E. Sewall, *American Jurist* (January, 1829) I, 35.

8. As late as 1833, however, it was estimated that 75,000 persons were annually sent to jail for debt — about 10,000 in New York, 7,000 in Pennsylvania, 3,000 in Massachusetts

174

and in Maryland. *History of the People of the United States,* by John Bach McMaster, VI.

9. *Mason v. Hale* (1827) 12 Wheaton 370; *Beers v. Haughton* (1835) 9 Peters 329; *Vial v. Penniman* (1881) 103 U. S. 714.

10. *The Great American Land Bubble* (1932), by A. M. Sokolski, Chap. XI.

11. *Niles Register,* May 9, 1835.

12. *History of the People of the United States,* by John Bach McMaster, VI, 335 et seq.

13. *26th Cong., 1st Sess.,* in the Senate, May 22, 1840, App. 797. See also especially *Social History of an American Depression 1837–1843,* by Samuel Rezneck, *Amer. Hist. Rev.* (July, 1935) XLI.

14. *History of Chicago* (1895), by John Moses and Joseph Kirkland, I, 98. Harriet Martineau, in her *Society in America,* wrote, II, 259–260: "I never saw a busier place than Chicago was at the time of our arrival (1836). The streets were crowded with land speculators hurrying from one sale to another. . . . It seemed as if some prevalent mania infected the whole people. . . . Storekeepers hailed them from their doors with offers of farms and all manner of farm lots. . . . A young lawyer realized $500 per day by merely making out titles to land."

15. *History of Modern Banks of Issue with an Account of the Economic Crises of the Present Century* (1896), by Charles A. Conant, 481.

16. *History of the People of the United States,* by John Bach McMaster, VII; *History of the Currency in the United States* (1915), by A. Barton Hepburn.

17. See list of 38 defaulters of the Public Treasury for $2,034,209, all from the South and West, except Samuel Swartwout of New York (Collector of Customs) for $1,225,705, and William M. Price of New York for $75,000, in speech of L. D. Campbell of Ohio in the House, August 12, 1852, *32d Cong., 1st Sess.*

18. *26th Cong., 1st Sess.,* in the Senate, June 21, 1840, App. 690.

19. *27th Cong., 1st Sess.,* in the House, August 10, 1841.

20. *25th Cong., 1st Sess.,* in the Senate, September 14, 18, 20, 21, 29, October 12, 13, 1837; in the House, September 21, 1837.

BANKRUPTCY IN UNITED STATES HISTORY

21. *26th Cong., 1st Sess.*, in the Senate, January 14, February 24, March 5, 27, April 1, May 12, 15, 18, 19, 20, 21, 22, 26, 27, 28, 29; June 1, 2, 4, 5, 22, 23, 24, 25, 1840. Congress adjourned for the session on July 21, 1840.

22. *26th Cong., 1st Sess.*, in the Senate, May 20, 1890, App. 803.

23. See speech of Thurman of Indiana, February 4, 1814, *43d Cong., 1st Sess.*: "On the great question whether there could be such a thing as voluntary bankruptcy, there was the greatest division of opinion among the lawyers of the country without regard to party; and here I may say in passing that it was only the speech made by Mr. Webster in support of that feature of the law, before he went into the Cabinet, which carried that feature of the bill and which afterwards received the sanction of the Courts."

24. See speech of Francis W. Pickens of South Carolina in the House, January 4, 1843, *27th Cong., 3d Sess.*

25. See Blatchford, J. in *In re Reiman* (1874) 7 Ben. 455, F. C. 11,673. Similarly Cowen, J. in *Kuntzler v. Kohans* (1843) 5 Hill. 317, said: "I read the Constitution thus — 'Congress shall have power to establish uniform laws on the subject of any person's general inability to pay his debts throughout the United States.'"

26. *26th Cong., 1st Sess.*, in the Senate, May 18, 1840, App. 793, June 5, 1840, App. 814.

27. *Life and Letters of Joseph Story* (1851) II, 330, letters to Webster, May 10, 1840.

28. *27th Cong., 1st Sess.*, in the House, speech of Henry A. Wise of Virginia, August 13, 1841.

29. *Memoirs of John Quincy Adams* x, 493.

30. *Life and Letters of Joseph Story* (1851) II, 407; see also Berrien in the Senate, July 22, 1841; Martin Fillmore, in the House, August 16, 1841, App. 480.

31. For progress of the bill, see *27th Cong., 1st Sess.*, in the Senate, June 10, 25, July 12, 22, 24, 25, August 18; in the House, July 12, 21, 31, August 10, 12, 13, 16, 17, 18, 1841.

32. See pamphlet by Albert Gallatin favoring application of bankruptcy law to banks in "Suggestions on the Banks and Currency of the Several United States" (1841) in *Writings of Albert Gallatin* (1879) II, 456–467.

33. *27th Cong., 1st Sess.*, in the Senate, August 18, 1841, and William R. King of Alabama said he had "never seen legislation so openly and shamefully disgraced by a system of bargain and sale."

34. *27th Cong., 1st Sess.*, in the Senate, Benton said: "I feel indignant that the American President should be so insulted," and moved that "the Sergeant at Arms take into custody 'those ruffians.'"

35. *27th Cong., 3d Sess.*, in the House, January 31, 1843, App. 70.

36. The third Whig measure was not successful — the Fiscal Bank Bill. It had passed the Senate, July 28, 1841, by a vote of 26 to 23 and the House, August 6, 1841, by a vote of 128 to 97, at which vote (the Reporter says) "the galleries resounded with plaudits, clapping of hands, bravos, hisses," etc.; it was vetoed by President Tyler, August 16, 1841, and on motion to pass over his veto, the vote was 25 to 24, and so the bill was lost.

37. *Memoirs*, x, 529. In the "Notebook of William Whitwell Greenough," *Mass. Hist. Soc. Proc.* (1910) XLIV, 33, there is this interesting entry: "Boston, October 3, 1841. Dined at Mr. Charles P. Curtis' in company with several gentlemen among whom were Mr. [Daniel] Webster, Mr. [Rufus] Choate, Mr. Mason and Mr. Gorham. Mr. Webster observed that he looked to the consequence of the Bankrupt Bill as very important to the country in one respect: that it would relieve thousands of excited people on the frontiers from embarrassment who heretofore had counted only on a war with England."

38. *27th Cong., 2d Sess.*, in the Senate, December 22, 27, 1841, January 17, February 15, 1842, when the bill to repeal being rejected by a vote of 218 to 23; in the House, a bill to repeal was debated, January 15, 17, 18, 24, 27, 1842.

39. *The Life and Letters of Joseph Story* II, 46, 104, letter to Judge Pitman, February 10, 1842; to John McPherson Berrien, April 29, 1842.

An article in *Law Reporter* v, in May, 1842, said that "the practical difficulties apprehended had been found to be of less consequence."

40. See speech of Lafayette S. Foster of Connecticut in the Senate, December 8, 1862, *37th Cong., 2d Sess.* See also

Senate Document No. 19, containing reports by Secretary of State, dated December 27, 1842, January 3, 9, 1843, *27th Cong., 2d Sess.*

41. See speech of John M. Berrien of Georgia in the Senate, February 24, 1843, *27th Cong., 3d Sess.*
42. Speech of Foster, *supra.*
43. See *Law Reporter* (October, 1842) v, 281.
44. See speech in the House of James A. McDougall of California, January 5, 1863, *37th Cong., 3d Sess.*
45. *Report of a Committee of the Charleston Chamber of Commerce*, November 24, 1841.
46. *27th Cong., 3d Sess.*, speeches in the House of John P. Kennedy of Maryland, December 28, 1842, of John B. Weller of Ohio, January 3, 1843, App. 70; speech of Henry A. Wise of Virginia, December 21, 1842; of Kenneth Rayner of North Carolina, January 12, 1843, App. 187.
47. *27th Cong., 3d Sess.*, in the Senate, December 14, 21, 27, 1842; January 11, February 3, 8, 24, 25, 1842; in the House, December 20, 21, 27, 28, 1842, January 3, 4, 5, 12, 16, 17, 19, 1843.
48. See decision given in full in *27th Cong., 2d Sess., Senate Document No. 19*, Vol. 2; see also *In the Matter of Edward Klein* F. C. 7865, reported in 1 Howard 277 note, being the decision of Catron, J. in 1843 in the Circuit Court reversing the decision of Judge Wells in the District Court (F. C. 7866) and holding the Act valid.
49. *Nelson v. Carland* (1843) 1 Howard 265, as to which see diss. opinion of Catron, J. in 3 Howard, p. 323.
50. See *Waller v. Best* (1845) 3 Howard 111; *Ex parte Christy* (1845) 3 Howard 292; *Nugent v. Boyd* (1845) 3 Howard 426; *Pulliam v. Christian* (1848) 6 Howard 209; *Houston v. City Bank of New Orleans* (1848) 6 Howard 186; *Peck v. Jenness* (1849) 7 Howard 612; *Mace v. Wells* (1849) 7 Howard 272; *Shawhan v. Wherritt* (1849) 7 Howard 272; *Colby v. Ledden* (1849) 7 Howard 626; *Oakey v. Bennett* (1850) 11 Howard 33; *Linton v. Stanton* (1851) 12 Howard 423; *Crawford v. Points* (1851) 13 Howard 11; *Buckingham v. McLean* (1851) 13 Howard 151; *Clark v. Clark* (1854) 17 Howard 315; *Bush v. Person* (1855) 18 Howard 82; *Commercial Bank v. Buckner*

NOTES TO PART II

(1857) 20 Howard 108; *Cleveland Insurance Co., v. Reed* (1860) 24 Howard 284; *Banks v. Ogden* (1865) 2 Wall. 57.

51. See in general, *History of the People of the United States,* by John Bach McMasters, VII, 44–49; "Federal Process and State Legislation," by Charles Warren, *Virginia Law Rev.* (April, 1930).

52. *Bronson v. Kinzie* (1843) 1 Howard 311; *McCracken v. Hayward* (1844) 2 Howard 608; *Gantley v. Ewing* (1845) 3 Howard 709. See also *Howard v. Bugbee* (1860) 24 Howard 461. Appraisal-laws of Arkansas and Michigan were held invalid in inferior Federal Courts in 1847 and 1845; see *Moore v. Fowler,* F. C. 9761, and *Rue v. Decker,* D. C. 12112.

53. *Chadwick v. Moore* (1844) 8 Watts & Sergeant 49.

54. *Von Baumbach v. Bade* (1859) 9 Wis. 559.

55. *Woods v. Buie* (1845) 6 Miss. 255.

56. *Hunt v. Gregg,* 8 Blackford 105; *Shaffer v. Bolander,* 4 Greene 201; *Mundy v. Monroe,* 1 Michigan 68; *Willard v. Longstreet,* 2 Douglas 172. See also Minnesota redemption Act of 1858 held valid in 1860 in *Stone v. Bassett.* Alabama redemption Act of 1841 held valid in 1846 in *Iverson v. Shorter.*

57. See *Hints for Relief by a General Law to Protect and Promote Amicable Arrangements for Extension and Compromise Between Debtor and Creditor* (1857), by Charles M. Ellis.

NOTES TO PART III

1. See *Law Reporter* (1858) XXI, 386, in which it was said: "The evils which arise from this unhappy conflict of laws are numerous and onerous. Every town in the United States has experienced them during the unhappy commercial revulsions of last year."

2. *35th Cong., 1st Sess.*, in the Senate, May 5, 1858, in the House, May 27, 1858. It may be noted that in the *33d Cong., 1st Sess.*, in the Senate, April 5, 1854, leave was given to introduce "a bill to authorize the recovery of the assets of a bankrupt where the same have been concealed or not specified in the schedule by him." This bill, of course, applied merely to bankruptcy cases then pending under the repealed Act of 1841.

3. But bankruptcy bills were introduced in Congress though not acted on. See *36th Cong., 1st Sess.*, in the Senate, by Robert Toombs of Georgia, March 13, 1860; in the House, by Daniel E. Somes of Maine; May 21, 1860; *36th Cong., 2d Sess.*, in the House, March 1, 1861.

4. *New York Tribune* said September 18, 1862: "$200,000,000 of indebtedness to our city was blotted out in a single night." President Lincoln in his Message of December 3, 1861, said: "There are no Courts nor officers to whom the citizens of other States may apply for the enforcement of their lawful claims against the citizens of the insurgent States, and there is a vast amount of debt constituting such claims. Some have estimated it as high as $200,000,000 due in a large part from insurgents in open rebellion to loyal citizens who are even now making great sacrifices in their patriotic duty to support the Government."

5. *38th Cong., 1st Sess.*, in the House, speech of Elijah Ward of New York, June 3, 1864; see also speech of Roscoe Conkling of New York in the House, January 7, 1863, *37th Cong., 1st Sess.*

6. *37th Cong., 2d Sess.*, in the Senate, bill by Lafayette S. Foster of Connecticut, May 23, June 25, July 14, 1862; in the House, bill by Roscoe Conkling of New York, January 28,

180

NOTES TO PART III

April 8, 14, 1862; bill by Isaac N. Arnold of Illinois, June 9, 1862.

7. The only exemptions of a bankrupt's property under the Act of 1841 were household and kitchen furniture and other necessary articles not in excess of $300 and wearing apparel of the debtor and his wife and children. It is interesting to note that not until 1902 did the Supreme Court finally definitely decide the question that this exemption clause did not make the law non-uniform. *Hanover National Bank v. Moyses* (1902) 186 U. S. 181.

8. *Suggestions for an Act to Establish a Uniform System of Bankruptcy Law* (1864), by Edwin J. James.

9. *38th Cong., 1st Sess.*, in the House, December 21, 23, 1863, February 15, April 23, June 1, 8, 9, 11, 1864.

   38th Cong., 2d Sess., in the House, December 12, 1864; in the Senate, December 13, 1864, January 25, February 9, 1865.

   As to the Jenckes Bill, see "Expediency of a Bankrupt Law," by J. F. B., *Amer. Law Reg.* (N. S.) (1864) IV.

10. See speech of John B. Alley of Massachusetts, in the House, March 25, 1866, *39th Cong., 1st Sess.*

11. See Delbert E. Paine of Wisconsin, in the House, April 21, 1868, *40th Cong., 2d Sess.*

12. *39th Cong., 1st Sess.*, in the House, December 5, 1865, January 18, February 8, 9, 14, March 27, 28, April 10, 16, May 17, 22, 1866. *39th Cong., 2d Sess.*, in the House, February 15, March 1, 1867. It is to be noted that the bill was first rejected, March 28, 1866, by a vote of 59 to 73, and on reconsideration was rejected, April 10, 1866, by a vote of 70 to 73; a new bill, redrafted as to its machinery to suit Conkling of New York, finally passed, May 22, 1866, by a vote of 68 to 59; and on motion to accept the Conference Committee's Report, March 1, 1867, by a vote of 73 to 71. It was stated by Paine of Wisconsin in the House, April 21, 1868, *40th Cong., 2d Sess.*, that the vote on the Conference Committee Report was at first 70 to 70 and that Frederick A. Pike of Maine changed his vote making the final vote 71 to 69.

13. *39th Cong., 1st Sess.*, in the Senate, May 23, July 14, 23, 1886. *39th Cong., 2d Sess.*, in the Senate, January 19, February 1, 2, 4, 5, 9, 12, 1867; in the House, February 25, March 1, 1867.

The bill was at first rejected on February 5, 1867, by a vote of 20 to 22; on reconsideration, February 12, 1867, it was passed by the close vote of 22 to 20.

14. On the other hand, John Sherman of Ohio said in the Senate, February 4, 1867, that creditors in Cincinnati and other commercial cities of the West were opposed to the bill, fearing that it would cause Southern real estate to be thrown on the market on forced sales and depreciated prices and as Northerners would be excluded by public opinion from becoming purchasers, they would lose their debts entirely.

15. *Amer. Law Rev.* (October, 1866) I, 206. The *Review* further stated that "The Boston Board of Trade was instrumental in defeating a similar bill in 1865, after it passed the House."

16. See *California Pacific R. R.* (1874) 4 F. C. 1062, holding the Act constitutional as to corporations.

17. Act of July 27, 1868, c. 258 (15 Stat. 227): *40th Cong., 1st Sess.*, in the House, April 20, 1868, speeches of Jenckes, Dawes, Paine, Maynard and Pike; in the Senate, July 25, 1868. An attempt was made in the House to extend this exemption from assent of creditors to a discharge; from January 1, 1869, to July 1, 1873, see *42d Cong., 2d Sess.*, May 28, 1872, H. R. 2475 moved by Ulysses Mercur of Pennsylvania. See also *43d Cong., 1st Sess.*, in the Senate, February 10, 1874, speech of Edmunds for explanation of Act of 1872.

18. Act of June 8, 1872, c. 339 (178 Stat. 334), *42d Cong., 2d Sess.*, in the House, June 3, 1872; in the Senate, June 3, 1872. See *Re Wyllie*, F. C. 18112 (D. C. in 1872) construing this Act.

19. "Homestead and Exemption Laws of the Southern States," by J. H. Thomas, *Amer. Law Reg.* (1871) x. See also description of State exemption legislation in *Denny v. Bennett* (1888) 128 U. S. 489.

20. Act of March 3, 1873, c. 235 (17 Stat. 577), *42d Cong., 3d Sess.*, in the House, January 20, 27, 1873; in the Senate, February 17, 18, 1873.

21. See *Guinn v. Barry* (March 31, 1873) 15 Wall. 610; *Edwards v. Kearzey* (1878) 96 U. S. 595. See also Note 61 *infra*; and see *W. W. Worthen Co. v. Thomas* (1934) 292 U. S. 426.

The following District and Circuit Court cases upheld the Act of 1873: *Re Jordan*, F. C. 7514 (No. Car.); *Re Jordan*, F. C. 7515 (Ga.); *Re Kean*, F. C. 7630 (Va.); *Darling v. Barry*, 13 Fed. 659 (C. C. Iowa 1882); the following Circuit Court cases held the Act of 1873 invalid: *Re Dillard*, F. C. 3912 (Va. Oct. 1873); *Re Deckert*, F. C. 3728 (C. C. Va. 1874); *Re Shipman*, F. C. 12791 (C. C. No. Car. 1875); *Re Duerson* (D. C. Ky. 1876).

22. *Amer. Law Rev.* (1879) XIII. See also the Attorney General's Report:

	Total	Involuntary
March 2, 1867 to Dec. 31	7,345	230
1868..............	29,559	443
1869..............	5,921	527
1870..............	4,301	884
1871..............	5,428	1,299

23. *Amer. Law Rev.* (July, 1873) VIII. "Rather than submit to such trouble and delay, creditors preferred to rely upon the ordinary legal remedies of judgment and attachment, though they might be obliged subsequently to restore such property as a preference. But even this risk was lessened by the amendment (preferences only with 2 months instead of 4 as in the Act of 1867). And even though a preference had been so obtained by actual fraud, yet the creditor would only be debarred from proving more than ½ his claim instead of the whole amount as previously . . . unnecessary litigation, exorbitant fees." *A Study in Comparative Legislation* (1893), by A. Whitney Dunscomb, Jr., p. 146.

24. *Ibid.* (April, 1874) VIII.

25. See also *47th Cong., 2d Sess.*, in the Senate, speeches of George F. Hoar of Massachusetts, December 8, 1882, and Benjamin F. Jonas of Louisiana, December 7, 1882, as to the scandalous administration in New Orleans. See also *54th Cong., 2d Sess.*, in the Senate, speech of Hoar, February 16, 1897: "We had down there in Louisiana, Judges, five of whom were driven from office from threats of impeachment, and I regard that history as the scandal of justice and the authority of the United States."

26. *42d Cong., 3d Sess.*, January 20, 1873.

27. See *49th Cong., 1st Sess.*, in the Senate, speech of Henry M. Teller of Colorado, May 24, 1886: "Let me say here as a matter of history known to every man here who has given the slightest attention to the subject that the panic of 1873 was precipitated and brought about by the Bankruptcy Act of 1867. . . . It can be proved by the records in Philadelphia that the great House of Jay Cook & Co., perfectly solvent the day that bankruptcy proceedings were brought against them, more than solvent, rich to a degree that we in the West regard as remarkably solvent, was brought down to utter ruin by the application of a simple creditor to put them into bankruptcy. . . . With it came a lack of confidence in the community at large everywhere and disasters that it took us five years to recover from. Impair confidence, and credit goes."

28. Act of June 22, 1874, c. 390 (18 Stat. 178), *43d Cong., 1st Sess.*, in the House, December 16, 1873; in the Senate, February 3, 6, 9, 10, 1874.

29. *Amer. Law Rev.* (April, 1874) VIII.

30. *Wilson v. Mudge* (1881) 103 U. S. 217; for other cases as to the nature of composition proceedings, see 227 U. S. 625, 628; 237 U. S. 447; 265 U. S. 269, 271; 273 U. S. 380; 278 U. S. 261; 289 U. S. 426, 437. And see the first case decided as to upholding the composition law in October, 1874, *In re Reiman*, F. C. 11673, per Blatchford, J.

31. In the House, Ephraim K. Wilson of Maryland and William J. O'Brien of Maryland, December 16, 1873.

32. *Amer. Law Rev.* (October, 1874) VIII; "The Repeal of the Bankrupt Act," by John Lowell, *Amer. Law Rev.* (April, 1876) X.

Another writer has said: "It would seem as if the intention of the lawmakers had been that the debtor who compelled the creditors to force him into bankruptcy was to be rewarded, while the debtor who voluntarily surrendered his property for the benefit of his creditors was to be punished." *Bankruptcy. A Study in Comparative Legislation* (1893), by A. Whitney Dunscombe, Jr., p. 149.

33. *45th Cong., 2d Sess.*, in the Senate, April 9, 10, 15, 30; May 1, 6, 9, 10, 1878; in the House, April 25.

34. *History of the United States from Hayes to McKinley* VIII, by James Ford Rhodes.
35. See also *29th Cong., 1st Sess.*, in the Senate, speech of Plumb of Kansas: "The law of 1867 was a miracle of extortion and oppression. . . . There was never but one case under that law as administered in Kansas in which the creditors got anything." Charles A. Culbertson of Texas, in the House, July 22, 1890, spoke of the "appalling and atrocious frauds under the Act of 1867"; and William C. Cates of Alabama said that "the stench from the administration of the 1867 law still rests in the minds of the people of the South." *51st Cong., 1st Sess.*
36. *53d Cong., 1st Sess.*, in the House, speech of Simon P. Wolverton of Pennsylvania, October 31, 1893.
37. *51st Cong., 1st Sess.*, in the House, July 23, 1890.
38. *47th Cong., 1st Sess.*, in the Senate, June 23, 24, July 5, 1882.
39. *47th Cong., 2d Sess.*, in the Senate, December 6, 7, 8, 9, 11, 1882.
40. *48th Cong., 1st Sess.*, in the Senate, February 4, April 8, 14, 15, 16, 21, 1884; in the House, May 19, 1884.
41. *49th Cong., 1st Sess.*, in the Senate, December 21, 1885 May 24, 25, June 1, 2, July 8, 1886.
42. *51st Cong., 1st Sess.*, in the House, April 11, July 22, 23, 24, 1890; in the Senate, September 19, 1890.
    52d Cong., 1st Sess., in the House, June 27, July 21, 1892.
    53d Cong., 1st Sess., in the House, October 4, 20, 23, 24, 25, 26, 30, 31, November 3, 1893.
    53d Cong., 2d Sess., in the House, December 5, 7, 8, 1893; July 16, 17, 1894; in the Senate, August 8, 1894.
    53rd Cong., 3d Sess., in the Senate, January 18, 29, February 18, 23, 1895.
43. See esp. Minority Report by Simon P. Wolverton of Pennsylvania, *53d Cong., 2d Sess.*, in the House, July 16, 1894. *Cong. Record*, pp. 7549–7556.
44. *54th Cong., 1st Sess.*, in the House, April 28, 29, 30, May 2, 1896.
    54th Cong., 2d Sess., in the Senate, January 28, February 16, 24, 25, 1897.
45. See esp. *54th Cong., 1st Sess., Senate Document No. 237*; see also *State Insolvent Laws* (1879), by Raphael J. Moses.

BANKRUPTCY IN UNITED STATES HISTORY

46. *55th Cong., 1st Sess.*, in the Senate, March 23, 25, April 5, 6, 8, 13, 20, 21, 22, 1897.
   55th Cong., 2d Sess., in the House, February 16, 17, 18, 19, June 15, 24, 28, 1898; in the Senate, March 1, 1898.

47. See Act of February 5, 1903, c. 487 (32 Stat. 797), *57th Cong., 1st Sess.*, in the House, May 2, June 17, 1903; *57th Cong., 2d Sess.*, in the Senate, January 21, 1903; in the House, January 26, 1903.
   See also Act of June 25, 1910, c. 412 (36 Stat. 838), *60th Cong., 2d Sess.*, in the House, January 29, February 6, 1909. *61st Cong., 2d Sess.*, in the House, February 23, 1910; in the Senate, June 6, 13, 1910.

48. *Buchanan v. Smith* (1873) 16 Wall. 277, per Clifford, J.: "Equal distribution of the property of the bankrupt pro rata is the main purpose which the Bankrupt Act seeks to accomplish." But see *Stellwagen v. Clum* (1918) 245 U. S. 605, per Day, J.: "The Federal system of bankruptcy is designed not only to distribute the property of the debtor, not by law exempted, fairly and equally among his creditors, but as a main purpose of the act, intends to aid the unfortunate debtor by giving him a fresh start in life, free from debts, except of a certain character, after the property which he owned at the time of bankruptcy has been administered for the benefit of creditors. Our decisions lay great stress upon this feature of the law — as one not only of private but of great public interest in that it secures to the unfortunate debtor, who surrenders his property for distribution, a new opportunity in life." Cf. also *Local Loan Co. v. Hunt* (1934) 292 U. S., p. 244.

49. *Canada Southern R. R. v. Gebhard* (1883) 109 U. S. 527.

50. For references to stay-laws in our history, see *History of the People of the United States*, by John Bach McMaster, III, 416–417; IV, 493–495; V, 161–166; VI, 624–626; VII, 18, 44–45.

51. See this view expressed in letter of Jefferson as Secretary of State to the British Minister, George Hammond, May 29, 1792, *Amer. State Papers*, Foreign Relations I. *Writings of Thomas Jefferson* (Ford Ed.) VII. See on the general subject, *The American States During and After the Revolution* (1924), by Allan Nevins, 336, 386, 390, 404, 525–526, 532, 537–538,

NOTES TO PART III

571. And see "Federal Process and State Legislation," by Charles Warren, *Virginia Law Review* (April, 1930) xvi.
52. *Elliot's Debates* i, 376.
53. *Grimball v. Ross* (1808) 1 Charlton 175; but see decision of the Georgia Court in 1815, holding a stay-law invalid. *The Supreme Court in United States History* (Rev. Ed. 1926), by Charles Warren, i, 355.
54. *Jones v. Crittenden* (1814) 1 North Carolina Law Depositary.
55. *Johnson v. Duncan* (1815) 3 Martin 380.
56. *Townsend v. Townsend* (1821) 1 Peck 1. See also *Richmond Enquirer*, July 6, 15, 1821, for a case in the United States District Court in Nashville, Tenn., holding invalid the stay-law. And see argument of G. M. Bibb on petition for rehearing of *Lapsley v. Brashear* (1823) 4 Litt. 44, 113.
57. *Brown v. Ward* (1822) 1 Mo. 209; *Bailey v. Gentry* (1822) 1 Mo. 164.
58. *Lapsley v. Brashear* (1823) 4 Litt. 44; see also *Grayson v. Lilly* (1828) 7 T. B. Monroe 6. See for Federal Court decisions, *The Supreme Court in United States History* (Rev. Ed. 1926) i, 642 et seq. See also *Fisher v. Cockerell* (1831) 5 Peters 248. See also speech of John Rowan, in the Senate, on stay-laws, January 3, 1828, *20th Cong., 1st Sess.*
59. *Bench and Bar of Mississippi* (1881) by James D. Lynch; see *Mass. Hist. Soc.* (1900) "Jefferson Papers," p. 338, letter of Christopher H. Williams of Mississippi to Jefferson, August 17, 1824.
60. "Homestead and Exemption Laws of the Southern States," by J. H. Thomas, *Amer. Law Reg.* (1871) xix, 137, 149.
61. *Edwards v. Kearzey* (1878) 96 U. S. 595. See also *Daniels v. Tearney* (1880) 102 U. S. 415, holding invalid a Virginia stay-law of 1861; and see *Terry v. Anderson* (1877) 95 U. S. 628; *Gunn v. Barry* (1873) 15 Wall. 610. See also *Moratory Legislation*, by A. H. Feller, *Harv. Law Rev.* (1933) xlvi.
62. *Sequestration Cases* (1868) 30 Texas 688; *Jones v. McMahan* (1868) 30 Texas 688; *Coffman v. Bank of Kentucky* (1866) 40 Miss. 29; *Goggans v. Turnipseed* (1868) 1 S. C. 80; *State v. Carew* (1866) 13 Rich. 498; *Taylor v. Stearns* (1868) 18 Grattan 244; *Hudspeth v. Davis* (1867) 41 Ala. 389; *Garlington v. Priest* (1870) 13 Fla. 559; *Jacobs v. Smallwood* (1869) 63 N. C. 112. Some States held their stay-laws invalid with

187

great promptness — see *Holloway v. Sherman* (1861) 12
Iowa 282, stay-of-foreclosure law of 1860; *Freebone v.
Pettibone* (1861) 5 Minn. 277, redemption-law of 1860;
Stevens v. Andrews (1861) 31 Mo. 205, stay-law of 1861;
Billmeyer v. Evans (1861) 40 Pa. 324, stay-law of 1861. See
also *Burt v. Williams* (1862) 24 Ark. 91, as to a stay-law of
1862; *Barnes v. Barnes* (1861) 8 Jones 366, on a stay-law of
of 1860; *Johnson v. Winslow* (1870) 64 N. C. 27, on a law of
1868–69; *Wood v. Wood* (1867) 14 Rich. 148 on a law of 1866.

63. *Hardman v. Downer* (1869) 39 Ga. 425; *Chambless v. Phelps*
(1869) 39 Ga. 386; homestead and exemption laws of 1868;
Hill v. Kessler (1869) 63 N. C. 437, homestead and exemption
sections of constitution of 1868; *Ex Parte Pollard* (1866) 40
Ala. 77, stay-law of 1866.

64. *43d Cong., 1st Sess.*, in the Senate, February 5, 1874. George
F. Edmunds of Vermont stated in the debate that in New
England such laws were held unconstitutional.

65. *Beverly v. Barnitz*, 55 Kans. 451; *Barnitz v. Beverly* (1896)
163 U. S. 118.

66. See list of these statutes and of the court decisions upon
them in 128 *Commerce Clearing House*, pp. 7802–7809, *Bank
Law Federal Service "L" Unit.*

67. See *47th Cong., 2d Sess.*, in the Senate, December 6, 9, 1882.
Against this provision, Senator Hoar raised the same objection which for one hundred years had been raised to
every extension of the scope of a bankruptcy law, viz., that
it was not "a known bankruptcy proceeding," and did not
come within the meaning of "laws upon the subject of bankruptcies," under the Constitution. "It is not a system of
bankruptcy within any legal definition." No Senator, however, agreed with Hoar on that point.

68. Act of March 3, 1933, c. 204. (24 Stat. 1467); Act of May 12,
1933, c. 25. (48 Stat. 41); Act of June 7, 1934, c. 424
(48 Stat. 911); Act of June 28, 1934, c. 869. (48 Stat. 1289)
known as the Frazier-Lemke Act. See *Continental Illinois
National Bank and Trust Co. of Chicago v. Chicago Rock
Island & Pacific Ry.* (April 1, 1935) 294 U. S. 648. For a
work opposing broad extension of the subject of bankruptcy, see *The Law Governing Liquidation* (1935), by Gar-
rard Glenn, and note to review in *Harv. Law Rev.* (June,

1935), XLVIII, 1463; see also *ibid.*, pp. 1430, 1435, and "Reorganization through Bankruptcy — a Remedy for What?" by E. Merrick Dodd, Jr., *Harv. Law Rev.* (May, 1935), XLVIII.
69. *Louisville Joint Stock Bank v. Radford* (May 27, 1935) 295 U. S. 555.
70. At least one Federal Court has held that Congress had the power to avoid all existing liens; see *In re Jordan*, F. C. 7514. Prior existing laws and attachments have been declared void by the Acts of 1867 and 1898. It must be admitted, however, that the constitutionality of the provisions of the Acts of 1867 and 1898, so far as they wiped out liens existing at the dates when the Acts went into operation, was never tested in the Supreme Court.
71. "The grant to Congress involved the power to impair the obligation of contracts." *Hanover National Bank v. Moyses* (1902) 186 U. S. 181; cf. Field, J. in *Legal Tender Cases* (1871) 12 Wall. 663; *Mitchell v. Clark* (1884) 110 U. S. 633.
72. See as to right to bind non-assenting creditors, note in *Harv. Law Rev.* (June, 1935), XLVIII, 1414–1428; see *ibid.* (May, 1935), 1100 et seq.
73. See, as to the limits upon the State Power, the recent case of *Home Building and Loan Association v. Blaisdell* (1934) 290 U. S. 398; *W. B. Worthen Co. v. Thomas* (1934) 292 U. S. 426; *W. B. Worthen Co. v. Kavanaugh* (1935) 295 U. S. 56.

INDEX

INDEX

Adams, John Quincy, 28, 70, 79.

Bailey, Joseph W., 138.
Bankrupt Act of 1800, 18–21.
Bankrupt Act of 1841, 70–79; repeal of, 79–84; constitutionality of, 85–87.
Bankrupt Act of 1867, 103–109; amendments of, 109–112; repeal of, 119–122; defects of, 112–114, 129.
Bankrupt Act of 1874, 118–119.
Bankrupt Act of 1898, 140–143.
Bankruptcy bills, in early Congresses, 10–19; in 1809–12, 22; in 1815–16, 23; in 1818, 23–24; in 1820–21, 27; in 1822, 28; in 1825, 39; in 1826–27, 40–45; in 1837, 57; in 1840, 60–69; in 1841, 70–79; in 1862, 98; in 1864, 101–103; in 1866, 103; in 1882, equity bill of Ingalls, 128, 152–154; in 1884, 129–130; in 1885–86, 132; in 1890, 134; in 1893, 134; in 1894, 138; in 1896, 138.
Bankruptcy Clause, in Federal Constitution, 4–5.
Bankruptcy law in England, 6, 34, 39, 118; in Pennsylvania, 6, 23; in Rhode Island, 6; in New York, 6, 24.
Banks, and bankruptcy, 43, 56, 58–59, 65–67.
Bayard, James A., 14, 15, 17, 18, 19, 21.
Benton, Thomas H., 8, 25, 58, 59, 62, 64, 66, 71, 72, 79, 84.

Berrien, John M., 39, 70, 85.
Broderick, Case, 141.
Buchanan, James, 31, 61, 72; Message of President, 95.
Butler, Benjamin F., 123.

Calhoun, John C., 55, 57, 58, 61, 71.
Class Spirit, 59, 132–133, 137, 139, 143.
Clay, Cassius C., 65, 67.
Clay, Henry, 27, 38, 50, 63, 71, 80, 159.
Clayton, John J., 65.
Composition, 44–45, 118–120.
Confederate States, bankruptcy in Constitution of, 6.
Conkling, Roscoe, 82, 97, 101.
Consolidation of Government, 41, 66.
Constitution, bankruptcy clause in, 4–9.
Constitutional objections, to defeat bills, 31–32, 74.
Contraction of currency, 55, 124.
Corporations, and bankruptcy, 64–68, 99–100, 107, 138.
Cushman, Joshua, 30.

Debt, imprisonment for, abolition of, 39, 52.
Debtors, combination of, to secure legislation, 37; number of, under Act of 1800, 20–21; number of, under Act of 1841, 81, 107; in 1860–61, 96–97; in 1867–71, 112. *See also* Bankruptcy bills, Vol-

INDEX

Pindall, James, 36.
Private interest, and public good, 33.
Railroad Reorganization Act of 1933, 154–155.
Randolph, John, 21, 32, 39.
Reed, Philip, 41.
Rhode Island, bankruptcy law in, 6.
Rutledge, John, 5.

Sergeant, John, 28.
Silver currency movement, 125–216, 135, 142.
Smith, Oliver H., 54, 66.
Smith, William, 10.
Speculation, in 1792 and 1797, 11–13, 38; in 1837, 52–55; in 1873, 114–118; in 1884, 130; in 1883–89, 134, 141.
State insolvent laws, 51, 76, 91.
State Rights, inconsistencies of advocates of, 43, 58, 65–67.
Stay-laws, 26, 51, 87–90, 146–152.
Stewart, William M., 105.
Story, Joseph, 40, 49, 56, 68, 70, 80.
Sturges v. Crowninshield, 24, 50.
Sumner, Charles, 107, 108.

Teller, Henry M., 132.
Thurman, Allen G., 119.
Torrey, Jay L., 134.
Tremain, Lyman, 117.
Trumbull, Lyman, 99.
Tyler, President, 69, 77.

Underwood, Oscar W., 141.
Uniform, meaning of, 62.

Van Buren, Martin, 40, 43; Message of President, 56.
Van Dyke, Nicholas, 27.
Virginia, real estate law of, and bankruptcy, 16, 21, 32, 33.
Voluntary bankruptcy, 27, 28, 39, 40, 60–64, 66; constitutionality of, 68, 75, 85–87; in 1866 bill, 104, 135–138, 141–143.

Wall, Garrett, 60.
Washington, Justice Bushrod, decision by, 22, 23.
Webster, Daniel, 38, 50, 55, 57, 59, 66, 70.
Whitman, Ezekiel, 35.
Wilson, James F., 102.
Wise, Henry A., 73, 83.

www.ingramcontent.com/pod-product-compliance
Lightning Source LLC
Chambersburg PA
CBHW021557210326
41599CB00010B/489